Geography of Dreams

RCR Arquitectes

Geografia de somnis

RCR Arquitectes Geography of Dreams

First published in Japan on January 23, 2019

Author: RCR Arquitectes
Publisher: Toru Kato
TOTO Publishing (TOTO LTD.)
TOTO Nogizaka Bldg., 2F
1-24-3 Minami-Aoyama, Minato-ku
Tokyo 107-0062, Japan
[Sales] Telephone: +81-3-3402-7138 Facsimile: +81-3-3402-7187
[Editorial] Telephone: +81-3-3497-1010
URL: https://jp.toto.com/publishing

Book design: spread (Tomoko Sakamoto and David Lorente)
Print: Sannichi Printing Co., Ltd.

Except as permitted under copyright law, this book may not be
reproduced, in whole or in part, in any form or by any means,
including photocopying, scanning, digitizing, or otherwise,
without prior permission. Scanning or digitizing this book through
a third party, even for personal or home use, is also strictly prohibited.
The list price is indicated on the cover.

ISBN978-4-88706-377-8

Geography of Dreams

夢のジオグラフィー

RCR Arquitectes

RCRアーキテクツ

Contents

6   **Resonance and Wonder**
       Works of RCR from Olot to the World
       Ken Tadashi Oshima

21   **Works**

22   Athletics stadium Tossols-Basil
36   La Lira theatre public space
54   Bell-lloc Cellars
74   Sant Antoni - Joan Oliver library,
       senior center and Cándida Pérez
       gardens
100 Soulages Museum
136 Crematorium Hofheide
170 Waalse Krook Mediatheque

203 **La Vila**
      Geography of Dreams

206 Site
208 Dream
241 Reseach and studies about the place
277 Existing buildings
277   Casa Pairal La Vila
279   Can Capsec
281   Cabana i Era
287   Bassa de La Vila
289   Magatzems i Estable
293   Molí de La Vila i Cabana

297 Global proposal in progress
303   Cloud Man and Cloud Woman
307   Humanitacle
311   Concepts of this territory
314   Site map
321   Arrival Space
325   Access Space
328   Research Center
339   The Air Stay - Fireflies
341   The Earth Stay
350   The Wood Stay
353   Paper Pavilion

394 Projects Maps
398 Profile
399 Credit of the works
      Credit of the book

目次

7	**共鳴と驚異** オロットから世界へ向かうRCRの作品 ケン・タダシ・オオシマ
21	**作品**
22	トゥッソル・バジル陸上競技場
36	ラ・リラ・シアター・パブリック・スペース
54	ベル=リョク・ワイナリー
74	サン・アントーニ──ジョアン・オリヴェール 図書館、シニア・センター、カンディダ・ ペレス・ガーデンズ
100	スーラージュ美術館
136	オフェイドゥの火葬場
170	ヴァールゼ・クローク・メディアテーク

203	**ラ・ヴィラ** **夢のジオグラフィー**
206	敷地
208	夢
241	この場所についてのリサーチとスタディ
277	既存建築
277	カサ・パイラル・ラ・ヴィラ邸
279	カン・カップセック邸
281	小屋と脱穀場
287	ラ・ヴィラの貯水池
289	倉庫と牧舎
293	ラ・ヴィラの水車と小屋
297	進行中のグローバルプロポーザル
303	雲男と雲女
307	ヒューマニタクル
311	このテリトリーの概念
314	敷地図
321	到着の空間
325	アクセスの空間
328	リサーチ・センター
339	空気の間─蛍
341	土の間
350	木の間
353	紙のパヴィリオン
394	作品マップ
398	Profile
399	Credit of the works Credit of the book

Resonance and Wonder
Works of RCR from Olot to the World

Ken Tadashi Oshima

Professor of Architecture
University of Washington

Resonance (conveys) the power...to reach out beyond its formal boundaries to a larger world, to evoke... the complex, dynamic cultural forces from which it has emerged...wonder (express the) power to convey an arresting sense of uniqueness, to evoke an exalted attention. [1]

Stephen Greenbladt

RCR Aranda Pigem Vilalta Arquitectes, based in the city of Olot surrounded by its wonderous volcanic topography in the Catalonian region of Spain, have long taken design inspirations from natural and cultural landscapes near and far. The exhibition "Geography of dreams" at Toto Gallery MA highlights their dynamic dialogue with Japan through the project La Vila and Paper Pavilion. Underlying the expression and experience of RCR's micro-cosmic space are fundamental connections between contexts. As Carme Pigem noted upon RCR's award of the 2017 Pritzker Architecture Prize being held in Tokyo:

Being...in Japan, brings to the surface other feelings that were awakened when we began our professional career together as RCR. When, for the first time, we experienced this country and its culture, with its exquisite perfection and love for nature, that has accompanied us since then. We know that the best decision of our lives has been to share architecture together. The second-best decision was to do this from our hometown, Olot....
We recognize that we love to dream and we love to build. For us, architecture is the art of materializing dreams throughout a long journey. And on this journey, we are pursuing architecture that contains the whole universe – just as the universe is comprised in the most delicate sheet of paper graced with the words of a poet, which help us understand it. [2]

The resonance inherent within RCR's work can be interpreted in multiple ways of mind, body, spirit. While resonance evokes feelings of closeness and familiarity, it also has the physical quality of sound and light waves reverberating within their work.

共鳴と驚異
オロットから世界へ向かうRCRの作品

ケン・タダシ・オオシマ

ワシントン大学建築学部教授

「共鳴（resonance）」は（中略）それ自体の形式的な境界を飛び越えて、大きな現実世界に到達する力。見ている者の心に、複雑で活動的な文化的勢力群の存在を思い起こさせる力である。それらの影響下にこそその物は出現したのだから。（中略）「驚嘆（wonder）」は、見る者の足をふと立ち止まらせ、独特だなあという意識を与え、関心を引き起こし心を高揚させる力である。（磯山訳）[1]

スティーヴン・グリーンブラット

スペインのカタルーニャ地方に、驚異的な地形に囲まれた火山の町オロットがある。このオロットに拠点を置くRCRアランダ・ピジェム・ヴィラルタ・アーキテクツは、行く先々で出合った自然風景や文化的景観を永らくデザインの源泉としてきた。このたびTOTOギャラリー・間で開催される〈夢のジオグラフィー〉展では、「ラ・ヴィラ」と「紙のパヴィリオン」を取り上げ、彼らが日本との間でさかんに繰り広げてきた対話に光を当てる。RCRのつくる小宇宙は、その表現といい空間体験といい、コンテクストの個別性を超えた普遍性を感じさせる。2017年に東京で開かれたプリッカー建築賞授賞式典に登壇したカルマ・ピジェムは、つぎのように語っている。

今回日本に来て、むかし3人でRCRを結成した頃に目覚めた感情がふつふつと蘇ってきました。当時初めてこの国を訪れ、その文化に触れ、以来、日本文化に備わった非の打ち所のない完成度と自然を慈しむ心がずっと脳裏に焼き付いています。思えば、この3人で建築に取り組むことに決めたのは、一世一代の大英断でした。これに次ぐ英断が、故郷オロットに拠点を構えたことです。
私たちはつくづく、夢を見ること、建物を建てることが好きなのでしょう。
そんな私たちにとって建築とは、長い道のりを歩み続けるなかで、そのときどきの夢をかたちにしてゆく術なのです。歩き続ければ、いつかは宇宙そのものを内包した建築に辿り着けるだろうと──それこそほんの一枚の紙切れでさえ宇宙を内包していると、ある詩人の言葉が教えてくれます。[2]

RCR作品が呼び起こす共鳴とは、知性・身体・精神の3つに関わるものだと考えてよい。人間の共鳴は対象への懐かしさや親しみの感情を喚起するが、いわゆる物理学でいう共鳴は音波や光波が作品内に反響することを指す。それゆえRCRのデザインは含蓄に満ち、「共鳴を呼ぶ抽象」に行き着くのだ、と建築史家にして批評家のウィリアム・カーティスはいう[3]。いわれてみれば確かに、RCR建築と風景との間にも、住民の個々の理解と共通理解との間にも、さらには国境を超えて異なる文化間にも

For historian and critic William Curtis, this creates "resonant abstraction" in their designs with many rich implications.[3] This notion resonates between their architecture and landscapes, individual and collective understandings between inhabitants, and broader cultural contexts transcending national borders. Yet the wonder of RCR's work can evoke "surprise mingled with admiration, caused by something beautiful (and) unexpected…"[4] As such, their work can seem both familiar and foreign, simultaneously evoking ancient and modern sensations in a stasis between dreams and reality.

The formation of RCR as the collaborative practice of Rafael Aranda (1961-), Carme Pigem (1962-), and Ramon Vilalta (1960-) brought together what they describe as an intimate "universe of shared creativity."[5] The three came together while attending the Vallès School of Architecture in (ETSAV) outside of Barcelona, which emphasized the realization of design inspirations. While they "built huts in the forest," Ramon noted "you couldn't just think of an idea and draw it. You had to tackle the challenge building it with a particular material."[6] Following graduation in 1987, the three returned to their hometown of Olot to start their own studio in the following year. The three soon gained international attention upon winning first prize for their reimagination of the lighthouse typology at Punta Aldea in the Canary Islands. Its abstract organic form attracted the interest of the firm I.C. Works to invite the young practice to visit Japan in 1990 for three weeks and participate in another architectural competition. For RCR, this experience imparted a deep impression for "a sense of perfection and beauty, effort and commitment that shines out in every corner, in a rich, lush landscape" in Japan:[7]

Japan had a big impact on us. We were very young back then in 1990. It's true, I think there is a very clear connection between its landscape and the landscape where we come from. Although Japan as a country is very big—you shouldn't generalize—I remember that the splendor of its vegetation seemed curiously familiar

to us. Its landscapes were close to our experience. The gardens of Kyoto, for example, have been shaped by human hands, as it's the case here: those places reflect another kind of humanization; they're not mere exercises in gardening. In Japan, sensitivity is something that is expressed on every scale, even in the smallest objects.[8]

They were also deeply moved by their discovery of traditional Japan through their "unimaginable overnight stay" at the Ryūsenin Buddhist temple at Mount Koya. As Ramon recalled:

I still have a crystal clear recollection of the night we spent in the temple in Koyasan, which almost no Westerners had done back then. We witnessed the complete transformation of the Japanese space: we arrived at night, entered our room and in the morning, the space began to change completely, opening up in its entirety. Suddenly, we found ourselves somewhere else. That made a very powerful impression on us. The same space, where we had come to sleep, was now a place for us to eat, to stay in. That experience opened up our minds. We also discovered something very exciting: you can achieve a lot with very few things. I'm talking about how important certain experiences are there, like moistening a pavement as a sign of reception. With just that, the action of pouring water on a stone, one felt something very profound. It's the kind of recollection that often comes back when we think about spaces and what we want to convey.[9]

RCR would continue its long journey through many visits to Japan over the course of the subsequent three decades underscoring shared values and deep affinities in the inspiration of nature in shaping daily life.

RCR articulates humanized landscape perceived through a heightened understanding of the drama of the fleeting moment and ongoing passage of time. Such a sensitivity is expressed vividly through the dynamic flow of the river, linking the thoughts of the Buddhist monk Kamo no Chōmei from 13th century Japan with those of RCR in their Garrotxa region in Spain:

共鳴するものはある。それでいて、RCR作品の与える驚異は、「ふいに美しいものを目にしたときの、驚きと感嘆の入り混じった感情」[4]を引き起こす。そんな夢ともうつつともつかぬ彼らの作品は、馴染みがあるようにもないようにも見えるし、懐かしさと新しさを同時に感じさせもする。

ラファエル・アランダ（1961年生）、カルマ・ピジェム（1962年生）、ラモン・ヴィラルタ（1960年生）の共同事務所として開設されたRCRは、当人たちのいう「創造性を共有する小宇宙」[5]となった。3人はバルセロナ郊外のバリェス建築学校（ETSAV）の在学中に知り合った。同校の教育では、着想したデザインを具現する力に重きが置かれただけに、ある課題で「森の中に小屋を建て」ることになると、「紙に描いた図面を提出するなどという生易しいものではなく、それなりの材料を使って石にかじりついても建てなければならなかった」[6]とラモンは振り返る。3人は1987年に卒業すると、故郷オロットに戻り、翌年には自前の事務所を開設する。ほどなくしてグラン・カナリア島の西海岸プンタ・アルデアの灯台のコンペに応募すると、灯台の類型そのものを一から見直した点を評価されて1等を獲得し、早くも世界的な脚光を浴びる。さらに応募案の有機的な抽象形態に目をつけたI.Cワークスが、1990年にこの若手事務所を日本に招き、3週間の滞在中に現地の建築設計コンペに参加させる。この経験が当人たちの胸に刻まれるほどに、日本の「緑豊かな風景にはおよそ隙がなく、そのすみずみまで美意識が光り、丹精が凝らされて」[7]いた。

　　日本にはそうとう影響を受けました。なにしろ1990年当時は、私たちも若かったから。お世辞ではなく、日本の風景には故郷の風景に通じるものが間違いなくあります。といっても日本は大国なのでひと括りにしてはいけませんが、それでもあの楚々とした日本の植生には、不思議と見覚えがありました。日本の風景にもどこか懐かしさを感じた。たとえば京都で訪れた日本庭園も、やはり人の手でつくられたという意味では当地と変わりません。これもまた一種の人間化というか、単なる造園とは違うんですね。日本では物の大小を問わず、あらゆるスケールに神経が行き届いている、どんなにちっぽけな物にでも。[8]

また彼らは、高野山の龍泉院で「想像を絶するような一夜を過ごし」て日本の伝統に触れ、深い感銘を受ける。以下はラモンの回想：

　　当時はめったに西洋人の泊まることのなかった高野山の宿坊で過ごしたあの一夜のことは、いまでも昨日のことのよう

に鮮明に憶えています。というのも、部屋のようすが一夜にしてがらりと変わるのを目の当たりにしまして。日が暮れてから宿に到着すると、そのまま部屋に通されました。ところが一夜明けると、部屋のようすがまるで違っていて、やけにすっきりとしているんです。一瞬、いったいここはどこだろう、と。まったく、狐につままれたようでした。寝るつもりで入った部屋が、食堂にもなれば居間にもなる。目から鱗が落ちました。それに、物がなければないなりに、たいていの望みは叶えられるんですね。感心したのは、日本では露地に打ち水をして客を迎えるんです。石の上に水が撒かれるだけで、なにかこう深遠なものが感じられる。以来、空間に何を語らせたいかと考えるたびに、あの時の記憶が蘇ります。[9]

RCRの旅はまだまだ続く。以後30年にわたり、彼らはたびたび日本を訪れては、なにげない日常を自然とともに生きる日本人の価値観に親しみと共感を抱いてゆく。

RCRは、人の手が加えられた風景の中にも、つかの間の出来事や絶え間ない時の流れを敏感に嗅ぎ取る。川の流れの描写には、そんな感受性が伺える。13世紀の僧侶、鴨長明の達観と、RCRがスペインのガロッチャ地方で到った境地には相通ずるものがある。

　　ゆく河のながれは絶えずして、しかも、もとの水にあらず。よどみに浮ぶうたかたは、かつ消え、かつむすびて、久しくとどまりたるためしなし。[10]

　　　　　　　　　　鴨長明　『方丈記』

　　フルヴィア川の水は滔々と流れることもあれば、よどんだり、灰色に濁ったり、青や緑に映ることもある……が、それはともかく。この世に水ほど変幻自在なものがあるだろうか。[11]

　　　　　　　　　　　　　RCR

鴨長明もRCRも世の無常を悟り、また双方ともに、自然の猛威の中ではこぢんまりと暮らすのが理想だとしている。

　　ただ仮の庵のみ、のどけくしておそれなし。ほど狭しといへども、夜臥す床あり、昼居る座あり。一身を宿すに不足なし。寄居は小さき貝をこのむ、これ、事知れるによりてなり。[12]

　　　　　　　　　　鴨長明　『方丈記』

Ceaselessly the river flows, and yet the water is never the same, while in the still pools the shifting foam gathers and is gone, never staying for a moment. [10]

Kamo no Chōmei 'The Hōjōki'

The water of Fluvià river can run, stagnate, be gray, green or blue...it doesn't matter! Nothing like water can transmit the multiplicity and the ability to transform. [11]

RCR

The fluid evolution embraced by Kamo no Chōmei and RCR is marked further by a shared paradigm of espousing the ideal of a minimal existence within the wondrous forces of nature:

Only in a hut built for the moment can one live without fears. It is very small, but it holds a bed where I may lie at night and a seat for me in the day; it lacks nothing as a place for me to dwell. The hermit crab chooses to live in little shells because it well knows the size of its body.... [12]

Kamo no Chōmei 'The Hōjōki'

Another essential aspect is the basic concept of architecture: as shelter for people. Not only in terms of form or function, but also emotionally. In other words, we are interested in arriving at the fullness of meaning, to the point where we make contact with the most intimate realm of the person so that they can have that feeling of shelter or protection. Ritual and mysticism have lost importance in the modern world, but not for us. We like to talk about beauty precisely because it is intrinsic and universal. Every civilization has cultivated beauty. [13]

RCR

This parallel underscores RCR's shared affinity for looking to the fundamentals of human habitation that they found in traditional Japan, especially as experienced early in their careers through their stay at the Ryūsenin Buddhist temple at Mount Koya. This experience would prove to be vital for reappreciating their own natural foundations back in Olot.

Early Work

The notion of primal shelter is embodied in the 2019 "Geography of Dreams" Paper Pavilion at TOTO Gallery MA, as well as one of their earliest built projects: (the 2x1 Pavilion and) Athletics stadium Tossols-Basil (1991-2012, p. 22) in Olot, Spain adjacent to the Fluvià River. Analogous to the ideal of the "ten-foot square hut," RCR's pavilions provide minimal protection from the elements of nature while serving to frame the fluid force of the surrounding environment. In the context of Olot, this is a composition of Cor-ten steel plates resting on the Tussols-Basil landscape to frame the adjacent athletics track stadium and soccer field. On the one hand, the placement of islands of trees within the tracks recalls the micro-cosmic, metaphorical landscapes of Ryōanji that they first encountered just before the start of this design. On the other hand, the athletics stadium situated within a clearing of an oak forest has been dematerialized to the elements of the track, overhead lighting towers, and minimal benches repeated to define stepping planes akin to the outdoor room of artist Robert Irwin's "Wave Hill Green" (New York, 1987) with a section of lawn lowered 18 inches and lined with Cor-ten steel to create a space for play and performance. Ultimately, the athletes competing and interacting with this natural landscape and environmental forces of Olot are the actors in this drama of everyday life for the audience to engage.

This design flows physically, metaphorically, and chronologically into RCR's Bathing Pavilion design (1998). Located downstream from the Athletics Stadium, the longitudinal volume is slightly curved to follow the sinuous course of the river and composed of Cor-ten and stainless steel walls, zinc roof and concrete podium structure that serve to highlight shadows of the surrounding trees. Further, the wedged volumes of the bathing cabanas further intensify framed views of the river landscape. While retaining the primal quality of precedents such as Louis Kahn's Trenton Bathhouse (1955) as a primitive bathing hut open to natural elements, RCR's pavilion has further evolved

もうひとつ忘れてはならないのが、建築とは人間をかくまうシェルターであるというごく当たり前の考えです。それも、形態や機能面に限らず、精神面でも人間を守ってくれるシェルターでなければなりません。ならば、その意味するところを最大限に汲むつもりで、人が完全に自分の世界に引きこもれる広さにまで範囲を狭めてゆけば、誰もが自分は守られていると実感できるでしょう。儀式にせよ神秘主義にせよ、いまどきもう流行りませんが、どちらも大事だと思います。私たちが美を語るのは、まさしくそれが固有のものでありながら普遍的なものだからで、つまりどんな文明もそれぞれに美を育んできたのです。[13]

RCR

鴨長明と比較するまでもなく、RCRは日本の伝統に触れて以来、人間の棲家が本来どのようなものであったかに強く関心を寄せてきた。ことにキャリアの早い段階で高野山龍泉院に滞在した経験が、故郷オロットの自然のありがたみを再認識することにつながる。

2x1 Pavilion
2×1パヴィリオン

Bathing Pavilion
水浴パヴィリオン

初期の作品

この原始の小屋という概念をかたちにしたのが、〈夢のジオグラフィー〉展の「紙のパヴィリオン」（TOTOギャラリー・間、2019）、ならびにフルヴィア川沿いにある最初期の実作「トゥッソル・バジル陸上競技場（と2×1パヴィリオン）」（オロット、1991–2012、p.22）だ。このRCR版パヴィリオンは、あの「方丈庵」にも似て、雨露をしのげる程度のものでありながら、あたりを流動する力に目を向けさせる。たとえばオロットなら、トゥッソル・バジルの大地の上に組み立てられたコルテン鋼板が、隣の陸上競技場とサッカー競技場の眺めを切り取っていたりする。ところでそのトラックの内側には、寄せ植えの木々が島のように点在するのだが、その光景には見覚えがある。そう、RCRがこの設計に入る直前に初めて訪れた龍安寺石庭の、あのメタファーを散らした小宇宙的な景色だ。かたやオーク林の空地に設けられた陸上競技場にはほとんど物が置かれておらず、あるのはトラックと頭上にそびえる照明塔とごく簡素なベンチのみ。そしてこの延々と続くベンチの並びというか、実質的には芝面を18インチ（約46cm）削って段差をつけたところにコルテン鋼を嵌めて観客席としたものだが、これなどはアーティストのロバート・アーウィンの手がけた戸外の部屋〈Wave Hill Green〉（ニューヨーク、1987）にそっくりだ。ともあれ、観客を前にこの日常のドラマを演ずるのは、オロットの風景や気候を時に味方につけ時に敵に回して戦う選手たちだ。

このデザインはやがて、物理的にも比喩的にもそして時系列的にも「水浴パヴィリオン」（1998）へと流れ着く。「陸上競技場」の下流沿いに横たえられたそのヴォリュームは、川筋のうねりに合わせて平面をわずかに湾曲させながら、壁のコルテン鋼とステンレスに、屋根の亜鉛鉄板に、基壇のコンクリートに木々の影を映し出す。さらに脱衣室の楔形のヴォリュームが、すでに切り取られた川の眺めをさらに絞り込む。脱衣所といえばルイス・カーンの「トレントン・バスハウス」（1955）の先例があるが、こちらの外気にさらされた原始的な小屋をRCRも本質的なところでは継承しているものの、しかしRCRはこのパヴィリオンをさらにカフェテラス「Pavelló Tossols」（トゥッソル・パヴィリオン）に仕立てるべく、「方丈庵」よろしくこれはという景色を狙いを定めて切り取ったうえでパヴィリオンの主役に据えている。

「バルベリ・スペース」（2004-）では、いちだんと理想のパヴィリオンに近づく。このプロジェクトは、オロット中心部にあった旧鋳物工場をRCRの仕事場に転用するというもの。かつて教会の鐘や聖像などを製造していたこの場所に、彼らは新規にパ

to become the Pavelló Tossols as a platform for dining al fresco in which the thoughtfully framed spectacle of the environment as described in the "ten-foot square hut" takes center stage.

The pavilion ideal further emerged within RCR's Barberí Space project (2004-) to create their work space through the conversion of an old foundry in the center of Olot. Within this space previously devoted to manufacturing church bells and ornamental sculptures, they created a free-standing pavilion around a low central meeting table, akin to the Japanese *chabudai* table, around which everyone sits on the floor for an intimate gathering with a direct view of the central courtyard garden. In complement to resonances with Japanese domestic space, the space creates the dimension of wonder with the floor level below ground giving one a worm's eye view of the garden, intensified by the height of the ceiling supported by slender cast steel pillars.

Just off the Barberí Space courtyard lies RCR's design of a fold-up toilet, at one with its natural surroundings. This is akin to the ideals of a Japanese toilet described as "a place of spiritual repose" within *In Praise of Shadows* by Junichiro Tanizaki [14] Rather than being hidden in an enclosed room, the RCR toilet shares ideals with Tanizaki in providing views of the sky and green leaves laden with the aura of smells and the variation of heavy shadows against light shadows. Within the office space, the lighting is kept low, as advocated by Tanizaki.

Such dark, shadowy spaces are found in their design of the Bell-lloc Cellars (2007, p. 54) located in Palamós at the head of the valley in the Ampurdàn region. Akin to the dewy path to a Japanese tea house that prepares one to leave the toils of the external world, the sloped path leads below the vineyards down into the ground to the tasting room and wine cellar to physically prepare oneself to focus on the precise tastes of the wine. Angled Cor-ten panels form a comb-like wall revealing rocks and allowing filigreed light to penetrate the underground spaces. One senses

the weight of the ground above and its thermal quality to stabilize the internal temperature. The scent of the earth and delicate light from narrow skylights above intensify the tasting of wine, all akin to the intimacy of a Japanese tea room. Here Tanizaki's "praise of shadows" resonate in this space: "And so it has come to be that the beauty of (the space) depends on a variation of shadows, heavy shadows against light shadows- it has nothing else."[15] This space composed of the primary elements of earth and light shaped by distinct oblique angles of the Cor-ten panels evokes a sense of resonance and wonder with Japan. This is a primal experience of "prospect and refuge," as described by Jay Appleton, with the perpendicular "refuge" spaces further leading to the "prospect" spaces of the testing labs looking out to adjacent verdant slopes[16]. Such elemental experiences are inherent to RCR's work and continues through recent work including their "La Vila" project and their design of minimal "air stay" cocoon structures in the forest.

Towards a Global Constellation in Space/Time: Mies, Japan, RCR and beyond

On a broader level, RCR's work has resonance and wonder with the work of great master architects such as Mies van der Rohe in consort with paradigms found in traditions of Japan. As Mies as asserted, "The building art is man's spatial dialogue with his environment and demonstrates how he asserts himself therein and how he masters it."[17] While Mies never traveled to Japan, many people have written about a dynamic dialogue, such as Werner Blaser's book, *West meets East: Mies van der Rohe*[18]. As Carme has recalled, "What I do remember quite clearly is my fascination with a visit to the Mies pavilion in Barcelona in our first year at the School. We had to draw it, and I was utterly absorbed by that plan, where everything fitted. I had discovered a world whose existence I had not known before. I also remember being utterly fascinated when I was younger by a house that I passed every day on my way to school."[19]

Barberi Space
バルベリ・スペース

ヴィリオンを建て、その中央の中庭を望む位置には、床に車座になって集えるよう、日本の卓袱台にも似た背の低い打合せテーブルを置いている。こうした日本家屋への共鳴があるかと思えば、驚異の空間もある。1階の床を地下レベルに落として天井高を増し、この天井を細身の鋳鉄柱で支え、虫瞰的な視点で庭を眺められるようにしているのだ。

「バルベリ・スペース」中庭のすぐ脇には、周囲の自然に溶け込んで目立たないが、RCRのデザインした格納式トイレがある。まるで、谷崎潤一郎が『陰翳礼讃』の中で「じつに精神が休まるように出来ている」[14]と述べた日本の厠のようだ。壁に閉ざされていないこのトイレなら、谷崎の望んだように、空が見え、青葉の匂いが漂い、陰翳もある。オフィス内もまた、谷崎よろしく照明が絞られている。

そんな陰翳に富んだ空間は、パラモスの「ベル＝リョク・ワイナリー」(2007, p.54) にもある。アンプルダン地域の谷はちょうどこのあたりからはじまる。日本では茶室の手前に露地を設けてせわしない俗世との距離を取るように、ここでも試飲室やセラーの手前にスロープを設けて客をブドウ畑の地下へと導き、その間に客が味覚に意識を集中させられるようにしている。斜めのコルテン鋼板が櫛の歯状に並んだ壁越しには岩が透けて見え、光が繊細な模様と化して地下空間を照らす。頭上に感じられる大地の重みと厚みが、地下の温度を一定に保っている。土の匂いや、スリット状のトップライトから洩れる仄明かりがワインの風味を増幅させる

ところなど、これまた茶室でしみじみと茶を味わう感覚に近い。谷崎が「陰翳を礼讃」する一節が聞こえてくるようだ。「事実、日本座敷の美は全く陰翳の濃淡に依って生れているので、それ以外に何もない」[15]。傾いたコルテン鋼板の隙間から洩れる光、そして土、というごく素朴な要素でできたこの空間は、日本に対する共鳴と驚異の念を引き起こす。ジェイ・アプルトンの「眺望－隠れ場」[16][自分の姿を見せずに相手を見る場所]理論が説く原初の経験よろしく、ここではまさしく地中の「隠れ場」を潜り抜けて試飲室に到達すると、ふいに「眺望」が開けて植物の青々と生い茂った斜面が姿を見せる。こうした原始的な経験を伴う点はRCR作品に一貫してみられる特徴で、近年のプロジェクト「ラ・ヴィラ」にしても、森の中に「浮遊する」繭型の構造物にしても例外ではない。

**世界各地の空間／時間に連なって：
ミース、日本、RCR他から浮かび上がる布置（コンステレーション）**

さらに視野を広げれば、RCR作品の共鳴と驚異の対象には、巨匠建築家らの作品も含まれてくる。そのひとり、ミース・ファン・デル・ローエには、日本古来のパラダイムと親和性があったとみえる。その証拠にミースはこう説いている。「建築とは空間を介した人間と環境との対話であり、よって建築には、人間がどんな自己主張をし、いかに環境を熟知しているかが示される」[17]。ミースはついぞ日本の地を踏むことはなかったものの、さかんに日本と対話していたらしいことは、ヴェルナー・ブレーザー著『West meets East: Mies van der Rohe』[18]はじめ少なからぬ数の文献が伝えるところだ。ところでカルマがいうには、「今でもはっきりと憶えておりますが、建築学校の1年生のときにミースの『バルセロナ・パヴィリオン』を訪れて、鳥肌が立ちました。課題でその図面を起こすことになり、すべてが収まるべきところに収まったプランに惚れぼれしたものです。当時は、そんな世界があることすら知らなかった。思えば、少女時代にも夢中になった家が通学路にありましたっけ」[19]。ミース作品にせよ、RCR作品にせよ、日本建築にせよ、その肝は、内か外かを意識させないほどに建築と風景とが溶け合う点にある。そんな流れるような空間の足元には、建築の基礎たる台座が据えられ、もしくは畳が敷かれている。空間の輪郭を浮かび上がらせるのは床材と壁材の質と種類であり、つまり「バルセロナ・パヴィリオン」ならオニキス、RCR作品ならコルテン鋼、日本家屋なら紙製の障子と襖がこれに相当する。とはいえ、空間の良し悪しは結局のところプロポーションで決まる。なぜならプロポーションは人体——すなわち「バルセロナ・パヴィリオン」に置か

Central to the work of Mies, RCR, and Japan is a seamless flow between the inside and outside, fusing architecture and landscape. Such a space emerges from the ground as a plinth, the architectural ground, or *tatami* floor. Space is defined by the quality and character of the materials of the ground and wall panels, whether it be onyx at the Barcelona Pavilion, Cor-ten steel, or paper panels of *shoji* and *fusuma*. Yet ultimately it is the proportions of the space as it relates to the human body – represented by the Kolbe statue at the Barcelona Pavilion or RCR's Man/Woman Cloud. Each of these spaces are interpreted subjectively by the human body, filtered by individual perception. As a component to the constellation, one could even see the sinuous plexiglass installation in the Barcelona Pavilion by SANAA as a further resonance of this dialogue. Just as Mies's work would resonate between contexts far and wide, so too would that of RCR. As Ramon Vilalta described,

Space has to be a catalyst that can open up a more transcendental facet with a more abstract dimension. Achieving that involves totalizing the body in that space. We spoke before about Japan. During that same period (1994 and 1996), Carme and I also visited the United States. Mies van der Rohe made a mark on us. Apart from his rigor and the undeniable value of his buildings, we were fascinated by what his architecture transmits when one visits it. When you enter a Miesian space, the body experiences a higher value. For me, it has that special ability to completely transcend the form and the building as such. When you go inside, it's as if the space were activated. It's an architecture that dignifies the person, beyond form and function. For us, that's what's really important. [20]

The embodiment of this activated space is expressed in RCR's Man/Woman Cloud, thereby underscoring the importance of experiences both felt immediately by the body and upon further reflection by the mind.

Further adding to the dynamic of West meets East, RCR photographer Hisao Suzuki presents his own vivid vision of East meets West. The photographic interpretation of modern architecture has certainly evolved and been multi-valent through history, from black and white to color, and views from multiple vantage points such as the landmark photocollage of the "Attack on the Bauhaus" (1932) by Iwao Yamawaki (1898-1987). While born and educated in Japan, Suzuki's love for the work of the expressive Catalan architect Antoni Gaudí (1852-1926) and food attracted him to Barcelona, where he has lived for more than 30 years. Suzuki's particular sensitivity and assiduous attention to capture the atmosphere and environmental conditions of an overcast sky, subtle light filtered through mist can be seen to resonate with the work of RCR through his photos or his commission of the design of the "House for a Photographer" (2006) that is yet to be built. As the partners of RCR have noted,

In addition to all (the) surpassingly distinctive signs of his photographs, which reflect the essence of... his Japanese roots, we need to value the nuances introduced by his more spontaneous, fresher Mediterranean experience, which confer on his photography and persona more richness and complexity: manifestation of an artistic experience between cultures, a combination that has undoubtedly led him (to) rediscover his roots in greater depth and intensity, his origins. And at the same time, this is what has given body to this mature work, without parallel, in the global context of architectural photography. [21]

An apotheosis of the confluence of all these forces can be seen to converge in RCR's masterful design of the Soulages Museum (2008-14, p. 100) in Rodez, France. While the museum and paintings by the abstract artist, Pierre Soulages, are situated in the artist's hometown, the abstract geometric composition of art, architecture and landscape resonate locally and globally. The whole experience is a series dynamic contrasts between dark and light, building and landscape, heavy and light, near and far.

The composition of minimal Corten steel boxes hovering above the sloping site is in itself a work of outdoor

れたゲオルク・コルベ作の裸婦像や、RCRの雲男／雲女——を基準にしているからだ。いずれにおいても空間は、人間の身体と知覚を通じて主観的にとらえられる。ところでこの世界的布置の1点には、先のミースの日本との対話への共鳴という意味で、SANAAが「バルセロナ・パヴィリオン」内に手がけたアクリル製のしなやかな曲線を描くインスタレーションも含まれる。こうしてミース作品がはるか遠方のコンテクストと響き合うように、RCR作品もまた共鳴する。ラモン・ヴィラルタいわく、

空間次第で、何かこう抽象的な次元にあって常識では説明のつかないような超越的な相が浮かび上がってくるはずなんです。それには、空間と人体とをセットでとらえる必要がある。以前に日本の話をしましたが、ちょうどその頃（1994年と96年）にカルマと連れ立って訪米もしているんです。で、ミース・ファン・デル・ローエにはひどく感銘を受けました。もちろんミースは自分に厳しい建築家だし、その建物は掛け値なしにすばらしい。けれどもわれわれの心をとらえたのは、建築から発せられるもの、その場にいる人間にしかわからない類のものだった。なにしろミースの空間に足を踏み入れるや、それがただの空間ではないことが全身に伝わってくる。ミースの空間は、それがどんな形態でどんな建物かを気にも止めなくなるくらいに超越しています。まるで空間が生きているように感じられる。まさに人間が尊厳を取り戻す建築であり、形態や機能を超越している。そこに感銘を受けました。[20]

この生きた空間を擬人化したのがRCRの雲男／雲女である。体験とはつまり、最初は肉体を通じてなされるが、のちに頭の中で反芻されて初めて意味をもつのである。

「West meets East（東洋と出合った西洋）」に触れたついでに、その逆の「西洋と出合った東洋」の透徹した眼差しでRCR作品を撮り続けてきた写真家の鈴木久雄に言及したい。近代建築の写真表現は時代を追うごとに、白黒写真からカラー写真へと進化しているし、また山脇巌（1898-1987）が代表作のフォトコラージュ〈バウハウスへの打撃〉（1932）で複数の視点を組み合わせたように、その内容も多義的になっている。日本に生まれた鈴木は卒業後、カタルーニャの建築家アントニ・ガウディ（1852-1926）の表現力豊かな作品に惚れ込み、現地バルセロナの食の魅力も手伝って、気づけばそこに30年あまり腰を据えることになった。鈴木ならではの感受性と不断の集中力が、その場の空気や状況をとらえ、陰鬱な空模様であろうと薄靄のかかった淡い光であろうと決して見逃さない。そんな鈴木自身もまたRCR作品と共鳴するからこそ、RCRの建物

を撮影し、RCRに自宅の設計「House for a Photographer（写真家の家）」（2006、未完）を頼むのだろう。かたやRCRは鈴木についてこう記している。

彼の写真にみられるこうした著しい特徴には、やはり自身のルーツにある日本が表れており、そして彼が流れ着いた地中海沿岸で得た経験もまた、写真に好もしいニュアンスを添えている。この長じてからの経験は、その写真と人格に深みと厚みを与え、さらには多文化を通じて培われた美意識をも顕現させた。もちろん異文化を知ったことが、自らのルーツなり起源なりを再発見することにもつながり、ひいては建築写真の世界に類をみない円熟の作品群をもたらすことにもなった。[21]

こうした世にも美しい邂逅が重なったのが、RCRの代表作「スーラージュ美術館」（フランス、ロデーズ、2014、p.100）だ。抽象画家ピエール・スーラージュの美術館と絵画はその故郷にとどまるものの、芸術と建築と風景の織りなす抽象的な幾何学は、この土地ばかりか世界とも響き合う。ここでは明と暗、建物と風景、軽と重、遠と近の力強い対比がたえまなく繰り返される。

斜面の上にはコルテン鋼のミニマルな箱がいくつも張り出しており、この外観自体が屋外彫刻めいている。このコルテン鋼が経年変化し、やがて定期家畜市跡地に設けられた公園と同化するころには、ここを介して旧市街と新市街とがなめらかに接続されるであろう。RCRいわく、大胆な幾何学的構成の「美術館が公園の中に立ち現れ、そして一帯を再構築し、秩序づけ、さらけ出し、すっきりさせる」[22]。斜面の上方からエントランスに向かうと、街並みとアヴェロンの山並みがぐっと迫ってくる。館内では濃灰色に統一されたギャラリーの床と壁が、黒と白で描かれたスーラージュの絵画を淡いコントラストで引き立てる。展示された絵画には、この背景に密着して微動だにしないものもあれば、ワイヤー吊り（ミースがベルリンの「新ナショナルギャラリー」で採用した展示方式）にされて重さを感じさせないものもある。濃淡のある影は、谷崎の「礼讃」であるとか、それこそ2018年に［同美術館の］企画展で取り上げられた日本の「具体」こと美術協会の作家などの抽象美術を想起させる。館内には、黒字に白で描かれた絵画とは逆に白地に黒で描かれた絵画専用のギャラリーもある。

RCRは日本との対話をさらに展開させるかたちで、ヴォイド（空隙）の概念から時間へ、そして磯崎新の指摘した「間-（ま）」[23]

sculpture. The steel forms age with time in consort with the civic Foirail garden, further forming a link between the city's historic center and new development. As a bold geometric composition, for RCR "the museum rises up from the park, it restructures, gives order, reveals and clarifies ..." [22] In approaching the entrance from above, views of the city and surrounding Aveyron mountain-scapes are experienced dynamically. Inside, galleries of dark grey floors and walls stand in subtle contrast to the blacks and whites of Soulages paintings. They are simultaneously solid against this backdrop and weightless as some are hung from wires (just as Mies displayed paintings at his Neues National Gallerie in Berlin). The range of shadows evoke Tanizaki's praise, as well as work of other abstract artists including the Japanese Gutai Group whose work was featured in a 2018 special exhibition. In contrast to white on black, complementary galleries feature Soulages black paintings on white.

RCR's dialogue with Japan extends further through their conception of void as it relates to time and the conception of "ma (space-time)" as articulated by Arata Isozaki. [23] As Ramon has explained:

The temporality of a work is related to how you work with the concept of time. Time is closely linked to space, in fact, time is what it takes you to travel through a space, or what it takes light to do that. Ultimately, time is measured via space. So if you manage to create a truly timeless space, your perception of time changes as well: although you are here, you feel as if you are immersed in an infinite time, where you can rest. How to express changes in the perception of time through the concept of space is a fascinating issue for us. We like spaces that persist over time – spaces that always remain in the present. [24]

This conception of space-time is embodied in their design of La Lira Theater Public Space (2011, p. 36) in collaboration with J. Puigcorbé. Situated in the small town of Ripoll, this remarkable public space weaves together threads of the past with the future as a new threshold new threshold in what RCR describes as

"the evolution and conscience of the humanization of *homo sapiens*." The urban frame sets the stage for the beginning of urban activity to spontaneously take place and extends out across the river valley almost like the "*hanamichi*" stage passage of the Japanese kabuki theater. It is both *local* and *global* as well as *primal* and *contemporary* in physically bridging landscape and cultures as the basis for inspiring human life from within daily routines. Here the spirit of the former La Lira Theater has been reincarnated as a covered square and stage for public debates and festivals. A steel structure with a lofty roof filtering light defines the site and acts as a proscenium framing the view of the Ter River and neighboring balconies, with an enclosed multi-purpose space below. The complex forms an urban artery; the space extends across the river as a steel louvered bridge with views to the surrounding mountains and water below. Glazed walls positioned according to subtle angles of the urban site reflect the activities of the space and its historical context, brought to life by the ever-changing environmental conditions.

Such a dynamic public activity space linked in space and time (*ma*) can be seen to extend beyond the borders of Spain to the Waalse Krook Mediatheque, Ghent, Belgium (2017, p. 170) in collaboration with Coussée & Goris architecten. Located at the nexus of the historic center and art quarter, this collaborative institution between the city and University of Ghent reimagines the role of a library to be a meeting place, site of cultural discovery, or place to engage innovations and technologies such as 3D printing and virtual reality. As part of the urban landscape, the De Krook brings together different urban paths and plateaus within the stepped structure as a central point of human interaction.

In balancing cycles of life and death, RCRs work continues full circle in the Crematorium Hofheide, Hieuwrode (Holsbeek), Belgium (2014, p. 136) in collaboration with C&G. This design of architecture in unity with the natural landscape brings together RCRs sensitivities born out in Olot, travels in Japan with the vivid character of the Flemish plain. In crossing over

の概念に到達する。これについてラモンはこう説明する。

　　作品に流れる時間、それはとりもなおさず、作者自身の時間概念です。時間と空間は密接に結びついており、その証拠に、人は時の流れに乗って空間を移動する、少なくとも光は時の流れに乗って移動します。煎じ詰めると、時間の長短を決めるのは空間ということになる。もし本当に時を超えた空間をつくることができたなら、時間の感じ方まで変わってくるでしょう。今ここにいるのに、まるで時が止まったよう、まさに悠久の時に身を任せるように感じられるかもしれない。時間の感覚を変えてしまうような空間というのは、なかなかに面白いテーマです。時が経っても変わらない空間—今ここにあり続ける空間って、素敵じゃないですか。[24]

この空間－時間の概念をデザインに盛り込んだのが、RCRの「ラ・リラ・シアター・パブリック・スペース」（2011、J・プッチコルベとの共同設計、p.36）だ。小都市リポイにあってひときわ目を引くこの広場は、過去と未来の糸を絡み合わせながら、RCRのいう「ホモ・サピエンスが人間としての自覚に目覚め、人間らしく進化してゆく」きっかけをつくる。都市の只中に設けられた舞台にはおのずから賑わいが生まれ、そして流域一帯に波及してゆく。その点では歌舞伎の「花道」に近いかもしれない。また風景と文化とを物理的に橋渡しすることで、当たり前の日常に刺激を与えるという意味では、ローカルであると同時にグローバルであり、古くて新しい。旧ラ・リラ劇場の精神は、立会演説や祭の会場に生まれ変わった屋根付き広場と舞台に受け継がれている。見上げるばかりの高い屋根から光の射し込むスティール製の構造物が、敷地をまるまるプロセニアムに仕立て、テル川と沿岸の家々のバルコニーの眺めを切り取り、さらに地下には多目的空間を収めている。広場そのものは街の幹線となる。つまり、広場はスティール・ルーヴァーごと橋と化し、遠くの山々を眺めながら、足元には川面を覗かせながら対岸へ渡る。やや屈曲した敷地形状に沿って立てられたガラス壁が、広場内の人影や周囲の古い街並みを映し出しては、まるで生きているように刻々と表情を変える。

人と人とを取り結ぶ〈間〉が賑わいを呼ぶこの種の公共空間は、その後、スペイン国境を超えてベルギーはゲントの「ヴァールゼ・クローク・メディアテーク」（2017、Coussée&Goris Architectenとの共同設計、p.170）にも出現する。旧市街とアート街の中ほどに位置するこのゲント市とゲント大学の官学連携施設は、従来の図書館機能を改め、市民が集まったり、文化に触れたり、3DプリンターやVR（ヴァーチャル・リアリティ）など最新技術を利用できる場となった。都市景観に連なる「デ・クロー

ク」は、その段を重ねた重層構造に街路や台地を取り込むことで人的交流を図っている。

生と死が循環するように、ベルギーはホルスベークの「オフェイドゥの火葬場」（2014、Coussée&Goris Architectenとの共同設計、p.136）において、RCR作品もまた一巡して元に戻る。自然の風景に建築を溶け込ませたそのデザインには、RCRの故郷オロットで育まれた感性と、日本で広めた見聞と、絵に描いたようなフランドルの平野とが併存する。沼地に浮かんだそのデザインは、大地をまたぎ、そして時間をまたいでRCRがかつて高野山の一の橋を渡って訪れた奥之院へと誘う。RCRは1990年に初めて訪れた日本で、弘法大師（空海）の御廟があることで知られるこの聖地に行き遭ったのだ。入定信仰によると、この真言宗の開祖は即身成仏を遂げ、現在もこの奥之院で深い禅定に入っているという。火葬場への道行きに付き従う風景には、虚と実とが混じり合う。たとえば捻れたコルテン鋼板がリズムを刻みながらずらりと並んだ外観に、古今東西の森の記憶が重なるように。そしていよいよ火葬場の中へ入り、死の現実と向き合う一方、身体は清らかな光に包まれる。その光を照り返すコンクリート面には、RCRが1998年の訪日中に訪れた安藤忠雄の「光の教会」（1989）のミニマルな壁面に通ずるものがある。地理的には日本から遠く隔たってはいるものの、この火葬場もまた、自然の力に任せてできた空間だ。生を死に到らせ、そしてまた新たな生をもたらすのも自然の力なら、さきに鴨長明の描いた、途絶えることのない川の流れもまた自然の力だ。

　　ゆく河のながれは絶えずして、しかも、もとの水にあらず。よどみに浮ぶうたかたは、かつ消え、かつむすびて、久しくとどまりたるためしなし。世の中にある人と栖と、またかくのごとし。[25]

　　　　　　　　　　　　　　　　　　　鴨長明　『方丈記』

RCR作品は、故郷オロットに限らず、東京、ヴェネツィア、ドバイ、ベルギー、そしてはるか遠くの地でも進化し続ける。どの作品にも共通して、人生という名の流転のドラマの繰り広げられる舞台が用意されており、そして舞台上では演者たちがめいめいに環境と響き合う。まさにここを舞台に、過去の記憶が現在と未来をかたちづくる。RCR作品を訪れると、その有形とも無形ともつかぬ空間から放たれる力に驚嘆する。夢に見たジオグラフィーが、目の覚めるような現実になっていることに。

the swampy basin, the design bridges the topography and also connects to RCRs own time traversing the Ichinohashi Bridge at Mount Koya to the Okunoin cemetery. The site that RCR first encountered on their first journey to Japan in 1990, is famous for Kobo Dashi: the founder of Shingon Buddhist is believed to rest in eternal mediation at Okunoin awaiting the Buddha of the Future. The landscape shaping this journey is both actual and metaphorical, as the hanging bent Cor-ten sheets create a rhythm akin to memories of forests, near and far. Inside, while one encounters the reality of death, one is surrounded by the purity of light reflected on minimal surfaces of concrete akin to those of Tadao Andō in his Chapel of Light that RCR experienced in their 1998 trip to Japan. While geographically worlds apart from Japan, this is a space shaped by the forces of nature as life gives way to death, and further bringing forth life as the flow of the river repeated once again by Kamo no Chōmei continues on:

Ceaselessly the river flows, and yet the water is never the same, while in the still pools the shifting foam gathers and is gone, never staying for a moment. Even so is man and his habitation. [25]

Kamo no Chōmei, 'The Hōjōki'

The work of RCR continues to evolve both at home in Olot and the far reaches of the world from Tokyo, Venice, Dubai, Belgium and beyond. Underlying this work is their design of a stage for the constantly changing drama of human life resonating with environments near and far to unfold. It is here that memories of the past shape the present and future. Within an experience between the tangible and intangible, one can discover through the work of RCR the wondrous power of making the geography of dreams a vivid reality.

1   Stephen Greenbladt, "Resonance and Wonder," in Ivan Karm and Steven Levine, eds., *Exhibiting Cultures: the poetics and politics of museum display* (Washington D.C.: Smithsonian Institution Press, 1991), 42.

2   Carme Pigem, Ceremony Acceptance Speech, Tokyo, May 20, 2017: https://www.pritzkerprize.com/sites/default/files/inline-files/2017_CarmeAcceptanceCeremonySpeech.pdf

3   William Curtis, *Between Abstraction and Nature: The Architecture of Aranda, Pigem, Vilalta (RCR Arquitectes)* (Barcelona: Editorial Gustavo Gili, 2004).

4   *New Oxford American Dictionary*, 2005-17.

5   Lecture by RCR, Global Ends Symposium, November 19, 2010, Architectural Institute of Japan.

6   "The Void, which Contains Everything: A Conversation with Rafael Aranda, Carme Pigem and Ramon Vilalta," "2012-2017 RCR Arquitectes," *El Croquis* 190, 2017, 15.

7   "2.2 Learning from Japan • Japan first years," *a+u* 542 (Nov. 2015), 40.

8   "The Void," (*Ibid.*), 25.

9   (*Ibid.*), 25

10   Kamo no Chōmei, 'The Hōjōki', *The Ten Foot Square Hut and Tales of the Heike*, trans. by AL Sadler (Rutland, VT, Tuttle Books, 1972), 1.

11   "1.2 Intimate landscapes of Rafael Carme Ramon," *a+u* 542 (Nov. 2015), 15.

12   Kamo no Chōmei, (*op.cit*) 17.

13   "The Void" (*Ibid*), 25.

14   Jun'ichiro Tanizaki. *In Praise of Shadows* (New Haven, CT: Leete's Island Books, 1977), 3.

15   (*Ibid.*), 18

16   Jay Appleton, *The Experience of Landscape* (London: Wiley, 1975).

17   Mies van der Rohe, "The Preconditions of Architectural Work," Lecture held at the end of February 1928. Fritz Neumeyer, *The Artless Word: Mies van der Rohe on the Building Art* (Cambridge: MIT Press, 1991), 299.

18   Werner Blaser, *West meets East: Mies van der Rohe* (Basel: Birkhäuser, 2001). Also see Yatsuka Hajime, "Mies and Japan," *Cornell Journal of Architecture*, Spring 2003, no. 7, 52-62.

19   "The Void," (*op.cit.*), 13.

20   (*Ibid.*), 25.

21   Rafael Aranda, Carme Pigem and Ramón Vilalta, "The Vision of a Look," *a+u* 504, Sep. 2012,112.

22   https://musee-soulages.rodezagglo.fr/en/museum/the-museum/architectural-approach/

23   Arata Isozaki, "Ma Space-Time" in Ken Tadashi Oshima, *Arata Isozaki* (London: Phaidon, 2009), 156-161.

24   "The Void," (*op.cit.*), 29.

25   Kamo no Chōmei, (*op.cit.*), 1.

1   Stephen J. Greenblatt, "Resonance and Wonder",
     in *Learning to Curse. Essays in Early Modern Culture*,
     Routledge, New York, 1990, pp.180-181.（磯山甚一訳
     『悪口を習う　近代初期の文化論集』所収「共鳴と驚嘆」、
     法政大学出版局、1993、p.261）

2   カルマ・ピジェムの受賞スピーチ（2017年5月20日、東京赤坂迎
     賓館）：https://www.pritzkerprize.com/sites/default/files/
     inline-files/2017_CarmeAcceptanceCeremonySpeech.pdf

3   William Curtis, Between Abstraction and Nature:
     The Architecture of Aranda, Pigem, Vilalta (RCR
     Arquitectes) Barcelona: Editorial Gustavo Gili, 2004.

4   *New Oxford American Dictionary*, 2005-17.

5   〈Global Ends〉シンポジウムにおけるRCRの講演
     （2010年11月19日、建築会館ホール）。

6   "The Void, Which Contains Everything: A Conversation with
     Rafael Aranda, Carme Pigem and Ramon Vilalta," "2012 2017
     RCR Arquitectes," *El Croquis* 190, 2017, 15.

7   「2.2　日本から学んだこと：最初に日本を訪れた頃」
     （「a+u」542号所収、2015年11月、p.40）。

8   "The Void," op.cit., 25.

9   Ibid., 25

10   鴨長明『方丈記』。

11   「1.2　ラファエルとカルマ、ラモンの内なる風景」
     （「a+u」前掲、p.15）。

12   鴨前掲書。

13   "The Void," Ibid., 25.

14   谷崎潤一郎『陰翳礼讃』中公文庫、1975、p.10。

15   谷崎同書、p.26。

16   Jay Appleton, *The Experience of Landscape* (London: Wiley,
     1975).（菅野弘久訳『風景の経験――景観の美について』法政大
     学出版局、2005）

17   ミース・ファン・デル・ローエの講演「The Preconditions of
     Architectural Work」（1928年2月末）。Fritz Neumeyer,
     The Artless Word: Mies van der Rohe on the Building Art
     (Cambridge: MIT Press, 1991), 299.

18   Werner Blaser, *West meets East: Mies van der Rohe* (Basel:
     Birkhäuser, 2001). 八束はじめによる以下の論稿も参照のこと。
     "Mies and Japan," Cornell Journal of Architecture, Spring
     2003, no. 7, 52-62.

19   "The Void" op.cit., 13.

20   Ibid., 25.

21   アランダ、ピジェム、ヴィラルタ「名匠のまなざし」（「a+u」504号
     所収、2012年9月、p.112）。

22   https://musee-soulages.rodezagglo.fr/en/museum/the-
     museum/architectural-approach/

23   Arata Isozaki, "Ma Space-Time" in Ken Tadashi Oshima,
     Arata Isozaki (London: Phaidon, 2009), 156-161.

24   "The Void" op.cit., 29.

25   鴨前掲書。

訳註：　既訳のあるものについては、できる限り既訳を参考にしつつ、
　　　　本稿の文脈・文体に応じて改めて訳出した。

Works

Athletics stadium Tossols-Basil   Olot, Girona, Spain (1991—2012)

"New architecture does not have to impose itself on the landscape: it has to coexist in it and make the most of all its beauty. The new landscape must once again become the landscape. Any runner can enjoy it." RCR

Mediation with the landscape

As can be seen from the Olot athletics track, one of the starting point of RCR's architecture is always that of mediation between human beings and nature. Landscape and architecture are conceived in an integrated way; nature is glimpsed, interpreted and enhanced in many different ways.

トゥッソル・バジル陸上競技場　スペイン、ジローナ県、オロット（1991—2012年）

新しい建築は、風景に対して押し付けがましい態度をとる必要がない。それは風景と共存し、風景の美しさを最大限に活かすものでなければならない。そうして新しい風景は再び、風景となる。ランナーたちはそのことを走りながら体感する。── RCR

風景との調和

RCRの建築の出発点のひとつ、それはこのオロットの陸上競技場のプロジェクトに見られるように、人と自然との関わりを調停することである。風景と建築を、統合されたひとつのものとしてとらえること、そこで自然は、いろいろな方法によって観察され、解釈され、そして拡張されるのである。

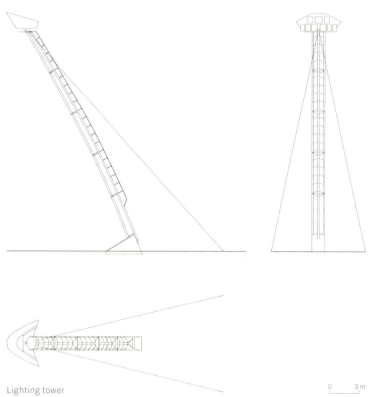

Lighting tower

0 3 m

Site plan

0   20 m

1.	Bicycle path	1.	自転車道
2.	Access ramp	2.	アクセススロープ
3.	Garden	3.	庭園
4.	Equipment building	4.	附属施設
5.	Gate	5.	入場門
6.	Veranda terrace	6.	展望テラス
7.	Access ramp to the stands and the locker room	7.	観客席と更衣室へのアクセススロープ
8.	Access ramp to the football field road and the locker room	8.	サッカー競技場と更衣室へのアクセススロープ
9.	Access to the locker room	9.	更衣室へのアクセス
10.	Stands	10.	観客席
11.	Running track field	11.	陸上競技場
12.	Road to the football field	12.	サッカー競技場への道
13.	Slope	13.	スロープ
14.	Lighting tower of the Stadium	14.	スタジアム照明塔

La Lira theatre public space   Ripoll, Girona, Spain (2011)

In collaboration with J. Puigcorbé

"Space appears when the boundaries are defined; it flows when it has continuity, and the onlooker perceives it when he or she performs the framing. The void is the defined space that the citizen breathes." RCR

The space

It is evident in all the works that space is the matter of RCR's architecture; it is treated in a sequential way, establishing a relationship between the interior and the exterior. This ever-present space even manifests itself in large voids, such as the Teatre La Lira square in Ripoll, Catalonia. Indeed, this emphasis on the qualities of space brings them towards the tradition of topophilia, or the ability to create happy spaces that, because of their forms and characteristics, work very well for people.

ラ・リラ・シアター・パブリック・スペース　　スペイン、ジローナ県、リポイ（2011年）

共同設計者　J. プッチコルベ

空間は、その境界が定められたときに現れる。それは連続する時には流れ、それを観る者はその枠を演じることによって空間を知覚する。このヴォイドは、市民がそこで息づくことによって定められた空間なのである。── RCR

空間

RCRの建築のすべての作品において明らかなこと、それは空間の重要性である。空間は連続的なものとしてとらえられ、その内と外の間に、ひとつの関係性を築く。このカタルーニャ、リポイに建つラ・リラ・シアターの広場において、空間は絶対的な存在として、巨大なヴォイドというかたちで現れる。このようにして空間のもつ質を強調することは、トポフィリア──土地への愛着──という伝統や、またはそのかたちや性質によって、人びとにとって幸福な空間を創造する力へと導かれていく。

Section

1. Plaza
2. Runway
3. Lobby
4. Ter river
5. Promenade
6. Workshops space
   Multipurpose room
   Exhibition hall

1. 広場
2. キャットウォーク
3. ロビー
4. テル川
5. 小路
6. ワークショップ
   多目的室、展示室

Ground floor plan

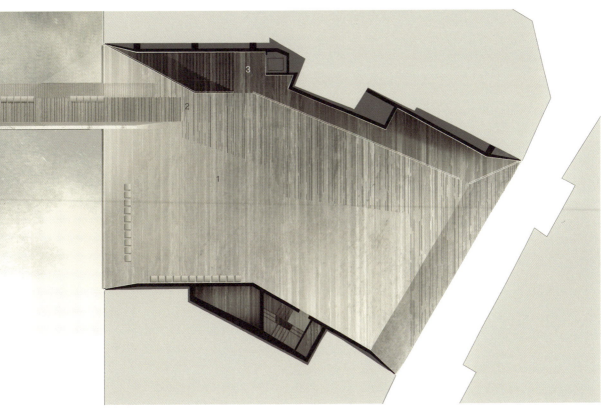

Bell-lloc Cellars   Palamós, Girona, Spain (2007)

"There is no greater calm than the one underground, nor any more time than the one marked by the rhythm of the sun. Going into the ground to rediscover the goodness of light and coolness. That the wine savours." RCR

Presence of Time

RCR's work is based on glimpsing, showing and treasuring the presence of time in its spaces. Its materiality is designed in order to incorporate time into it, in the same way as Corten steel does. At the Bell-Lloc wineries in Palamós, Catalonia, this passing of time is expressed by the cycles of nature in the vineyards and by how it is perceived in the interior, with shafts of natural light and shadows emanating from and cast by the sun and the moon, which gradually shift direction, as if inside a temple.

ベル=リョク・ワイナリー　スペイン、ジローナ県、パラモス (2007年)

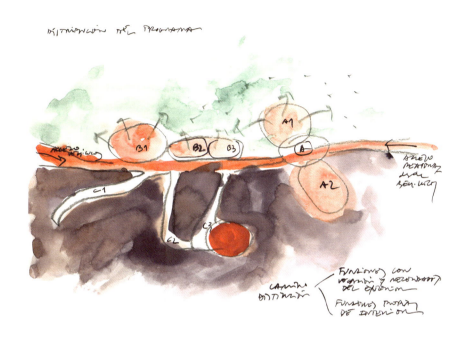

地下よりも静かな場所はない、そして太陽が刻む時間以上に明確なリズムはない。地下に下りて、光と、涼しさのありがたさを再び発見すること。それこそが、ここで熟成されるワインが堪能しているものなのだ。── RCR

時間の存在

RCRはその作品において、空間を見つめること、そしてそこに宿る時間の存在を慈しみ、それを表現することを大切にする。そして素材性というものを、時間を織り込んでいくものとして設計する。コールテン鋼の経年変化のように。カタルーニャのパラモスに建つこのベル=リョク・ワイナリーでは、そのような時間の経過が、葡萄畑を巡る季節の循環として、あるいはその室内においては自然光とそれがつくる影として、表現されている。まるで聖堂の中のように、太陽と月が落とす光の柱の軌跡が、ゆっくりと移動していく。

1. Tractor access ramp
2. Unloading area and inicial work space
3. Fermentation room
4. Internal passway
5. Pedestrian access ramp
6. Porch, various activities
7. Exterior space
8. Workshop
9. Laboratory and fractionation, bottling and labeling line
10. Light-ventilation space
11. Auditorium-multipurpose room
12. Storage
13. Tasting room
14. Bottle cellar
15. Bota bag cellar
16. Machines storage, packaging and installations space
17. WC
18. Changing room
19. Installations room

1. トラクター用搬入路
2. 荷降ろし場
3. 発酵室
4. 従業員用通路
5. 歩行者入り口
6. ポーチ、各種作業場
7. 屋外空間
8. ワークショップ
9. 研究所および分別、瓶詰、ラベル貼りライン
10. 採光、換気スペース
11. オーディトリアム、多目的室
12. 倉庫
13. テイスティングルーム
14. ボトル用セラー
15. 革袋用セラー
16. 機械室・倉庫
17. 洗面所
18. 更衣室
19. 設備室

Plan
0   5 m

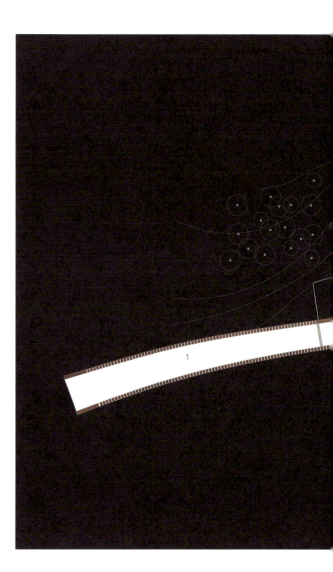

Section
0   2 m

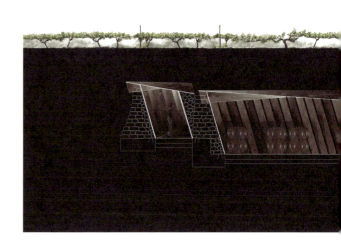

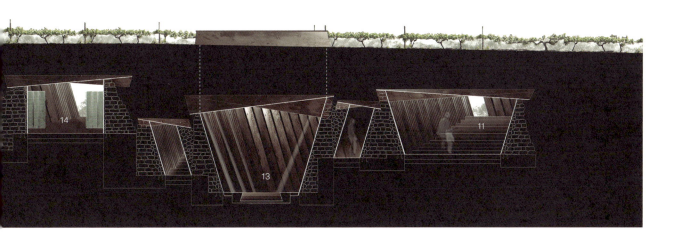

Sant Antoni - Joan Oliver library, senior center and Cándida Pérez gardens
Sant Antoni neighborhood, Barcelona, Spain (2007)

"The multilayered city needs social nexus to make the human richness of generations and exchanges palpable, like a sponge woven from voids. And children should play." RCR

The public and social function

RCR has a particular interest in public buildings and their social function. A work like the library and centre for the elderly in Barcelona are evidence of that: it is based on the person who walks, perceives, and uses the services of the building. The visuals and the relationships between people are strengthened, bringing together three activities (reading, recreation in the garden and the activities of the elders) and fostering encounters between generations. A kind of forest is generated, dense and transparent, full of atmospheres. It was also an occasion for a new interpretation of the Eixample district designed by Ildefons Cerdà.

サン・アントーニ —— ジョアン・オリヴェール図書館、シニア・センター、カンディダ・ペレス・ガーデンズ
スペイン、バルセロナ、サン・アントーニ地区（2007年）

多層な都市においては、ヴォイドを編んで作ったスポンジのように、多様な世代の人間の豊かさとその交流を感じられるような社会的なつながりが必要だ。そして、子供の遊ぶ場が必要だ。—— RCR

公的、社会的な機能

RCRは、公共建築とそれがもつ社会的な機能に対して特別な感心を抱いている。そのことが、このバルセロナに建つ図書館と高齢者のためのセンターにも強く現れている。この建物は、ここを歩き、眺め、サービスを享受する人の目線で設計されており、ここで行われる3つの主な活動（図書館で本を読む、中庭で遊ぶ、高齢者たちが憩う）は、多様な世代のユーザーたちの出会い、関わり合いを促している。ここは濃密で透明で多様な空気感をまとった、ある種の森なのだ。そしてイルフォンソ・セルダが設計した拡張地区の、新たな解釈に対する提案にもなっている（ブロックを閉じる代わりに空間的にも機能的にも開かれた中庭がつくられている）。

1. Access
2. Entrance hall
3. Principal stairs
4. EV
5. Borrowins counter / control of magazines & newspaper area
6. Ticket
7. Information counter
8. Magazines & newspaper area
9. Exit/emergency stairs
10. Machine room
11. Locker room
12. Public telephone
13. Direction/management
14. Bar area
15. Porch
16. Internet space
17. Drink machine
18. Storage for cleaning
19. Sanitary service
20. Event room
21. Workshop space
22. Storage
23. Event room
24. Annex space
25. Sound room
26. Working space
27. Break room for workers
28. Playing room
29. Gym
30. Changing room
31. Office
32. Classes and workshops I
33. Classes and workshops II
34. Computer room
35. EV Machine room
36. Reading space for kids
37. Knowledge fund area
38. Imagination fund area
39. Kitchen garden tool storage
40. Kitchen garden
41. General fund area
42. Self-service photocopy machine
43. Exhibition space
44. Machine room
45. Music and imagination fund area
46. Garden
47. Kids' area
48. Benches

A. Hedera helix var. baltica Ivy
B. Parthenocissus Ivy
C. African Tamarix
D. Populus Nigra Italica - Black poplar

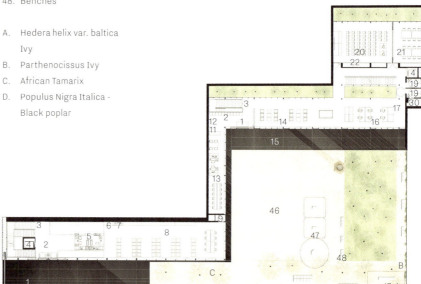

Ground floor plan

Basement floor plan

1.	出入り口	27.	職員休憩室
2.	エントランスホール	28.	遊具
3.	主階段	29.	ジム
4.	エレベータ	30.	更衣室
5.	図書貸出、雑誌、新聞閲覧カウンター	31.	オフィス
		32.	教室、ワークショップ I
6.	チケットカウンター	33.	教室、ワークショップ II
7.	情報カウンター	34.	コンピュータ室
8.	雑誌、新聞閲覧エリア	35.	エレベータ機械室
9.	出口、避難階段	36.	子供用読書室
10.	機械室	37.	知識のエリア
11.	ロッカー	38.	想像のエリア
12.	公衆電話	39.	菜園用農具保管室
13.	館長室、管理運営室	40.	菜園
14.	カフェ	41.	一般エリア
15.	ポーチ	42.	コピー機
16.	インターネット接続エリア	43.	展示スペース
17.	自動販売機	44.	機械室
18.	清掃用具置場	45.	音楽、想像のエリア
19.	サニタリーサービス	46.	ガーデン
20.	イベント室	47.	キッズエリア
21.	ワークショップ室	48.	ベンチ
22.	倉庫		
23.	イベント室	A.	セイヨウキヅタ
24.	居室拡張エリア	B.	ツタ
25.	防音室	C.	アフリカ・ギョリュウ
26.	作業室	D.	セイヨウハコヤナギ

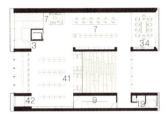

Third floor plan

Second floor plan

First floor plan

Section

1. Access
2. Garden
3. Imagination fund area
4. Music and imagination fund area
5. General fund area
6. Break room for workers
7. Working space
8. Annex space
9. Event room

1. 出入り口
2. ガーデン
3. 想像貯蔵エリア
4. 音楽、想像貯蔵エリア
5. 一般貯蔵エリア
6. 職員休憩室
7. 作業室
8. 居室拡張エリア
9. イベント室

Soulages Museum   Rodez, France (2014)

In collaboration with: G. Trégouët (RCR Arquitectes)

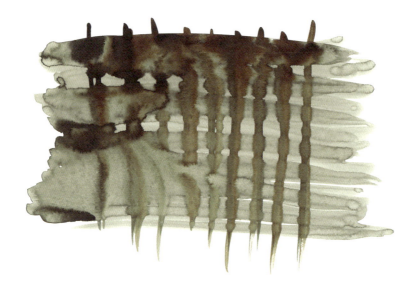

"The architecture that puts order into our activities can also put order into paintings in well-placed boxes emerging from the earth and laid out with air between them. They should allow people to see and allow themselves to be seen." RCR

Structure and materiality

In RCR's work, the architecture is the structure. Moreover, the essence of each intervention is matter, materials and materiality. Each work entails a close-up vision from the haptic, tactile, rough, perceptive character. The Musée Soulages in Rodez, France, with the interior spaces and volumes made and illuminated specifically for the artworks, is an outstanding demonstration of that.

スーラージュ美術館　　フランス、ロデーズ（2014年）

G. トレグエット（RCRアーキテクツ）との協働

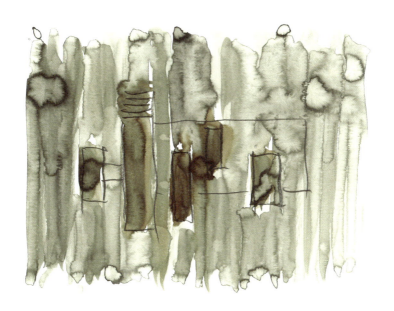

われわれの活動に秩序をもたらす建築は、絵画にとっても秩序をもたらすことができるだろう。それは大地から現れ出て、間隔を置いて適切に配された複数の箱である。人びとが絵画を鑑賞できるように、そして人びとが互いの存在をもよく見ることができるように。── RCR

構造と素材

RCRの作品において、建築と構造は同義である。さらに、すべての建造物にとって最も本質的なのが、物質、素材、そして質感である。それぞれの作品からは、触覚的で、ザラザラとした、知覚に訴える性質を感じ取ることができる。フランスのロデーズに建つこのスーラージュ美術館においては、その展示作品のために特別に設えられ、調光された室内空間とヴォリュームが、そのことを如実に示している。

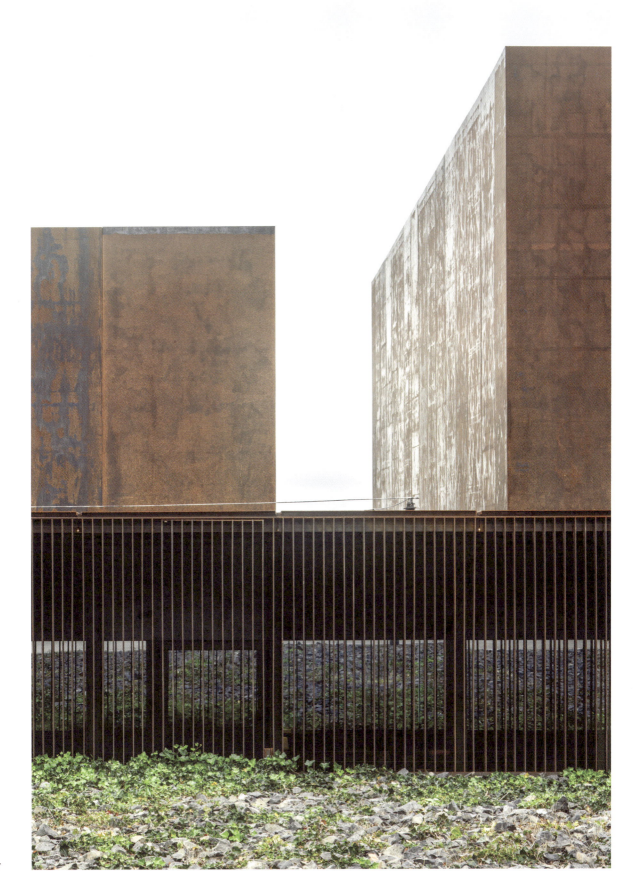

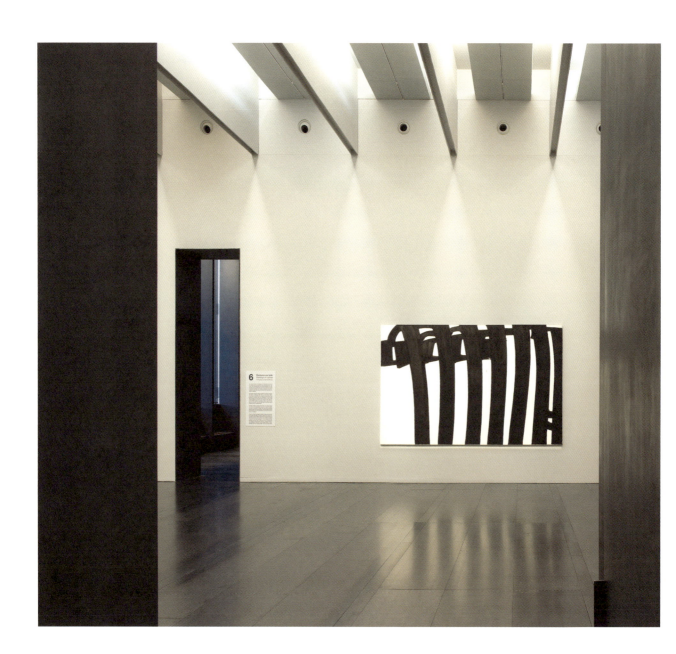

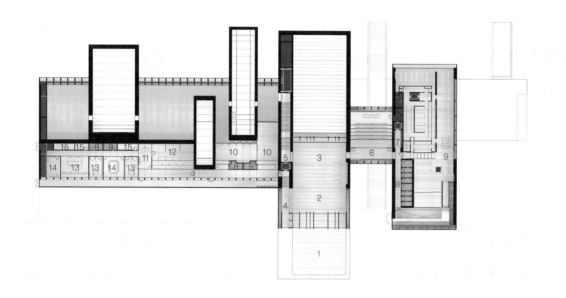

Access plan

Exhibition halls plan

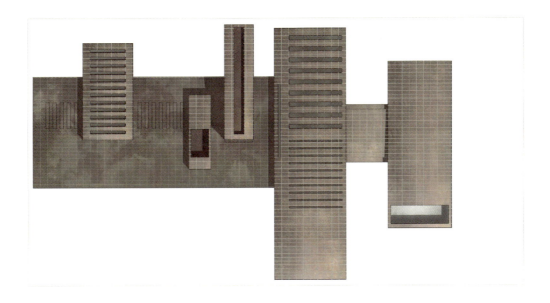

Rooftop plan

1. Porch-access
2. Entrance hall
3. Información center
4. Reception counter
5. Exhibition access stairs
6. Auditorium
7. Ticket
8. WC
9. Restaurant
10. Educational ateliers
11. Secretary
12. Consultation and research room
13. Management office
14. Meeting room
15. Storage
16. Hall
17. Temporary exhibition hall
18. Conques l'atelier
19. Initial works
20. Space available to the artist
21. Etchings-lithographs-serigraphs
22. Works on canvas
23. Works on paper

1. アクセスポーチ
2. エントランスホール
3. インフォメーション
4. 受付
5. 展示室に至る階段
6. オーディトリアム
7. チケット売場
8. 洗面所
9. レストラン
10. 学習アトリエ
11. 秘書室
12. 相談、研究室
13. 管理事務所
14. 会議室
15. 倉庫
16. 展示室
17. 企画展示室
18. コンカスのアトリエ
19. 初期作品
20. アーティスト特別専用室
21. エッチング、リトグラフ、シルクスクリーン作品
22. キャンバス作品
23. 紙作品

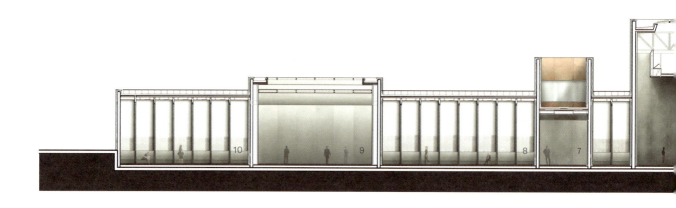
Longitudinal section

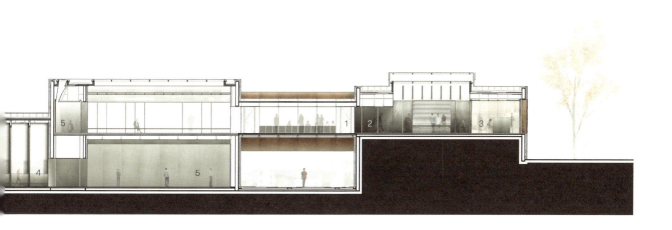

1.	Auditorium	1.	オーディトリアム
2.	Ticket	2.	チケット売場
3.	Restaurant	3.	レストラン
4.	Hall	4.	展示室
5.	Temporary exhibition hall	5.	企画展示室
6.	Conques l'atelier	6.	コンカスのアトリエ
7.	Initial works	7.	初期作品
8.	Space available to the artist	8.	アーティスト特別専用室
9.	Works on canvas	9.	キャンバス作品
10.	Works on paper	10.	紙作品

Crematorium Hofheide   Nieuwrode (Holsbeek), Belgium (2014)
Associated architects: Coussée & Goris Architecten

"Spirituality is an invisible path between the earth and the sky, a network made from horizons and verticalities conjugated with shadows and light. There is no belonging, but rather exchanges." RCR

The System

Each of RCR's works holds a set of characteristics and gradually evolves, making a synthesis of them and taking a new step forward. There is a method, a system in which complexity is resolved: the live relationship with the landscape; the composition based on spatial sequences; the social, spiritual and community function; the passing of time; the powerful presence of structure, volume and materiality, and the quest for lightness, transparency, immateriality and, at the same time, their contrast, something telluric and tectonic. All of this is synthesised in works like the crematorium in Belgium.

オフェイドゥの火葬場　　ベルギー、ホルスベーク、（2014年）
Coussée & Goris Architectenとの共同設計

精神性、スピリチュアリティというものは、大地と天空の間をつなぐ目に見えない道、光と影が織りなす地平と垂直性から成るネットワークなのだ。そこには所属や所有といったものは存在せず、むしろ交換があるのだ。── RCR

システム

RCRの作品には共通して、徐々に進化しながらまとまって次の新たな一歩へと踏み出す、という一連の特徴がある。そこには方法論があり、複雑さを解消するシステムがあり、風景との間に生きた関係があり、空間の連続に基づく構成があり、社会的、精神的なコミュニティのための機能がある。時間の経過、構造やボリューム、物質性の圧倒的な存在感、そして軽さや透明性、非物質性への希求。同時にそれとは反対に、大地から生まれたような地殻的な性質をもあわせもつ。これらのすべてが、このベルギーの火葬場の中に統合されているのである。

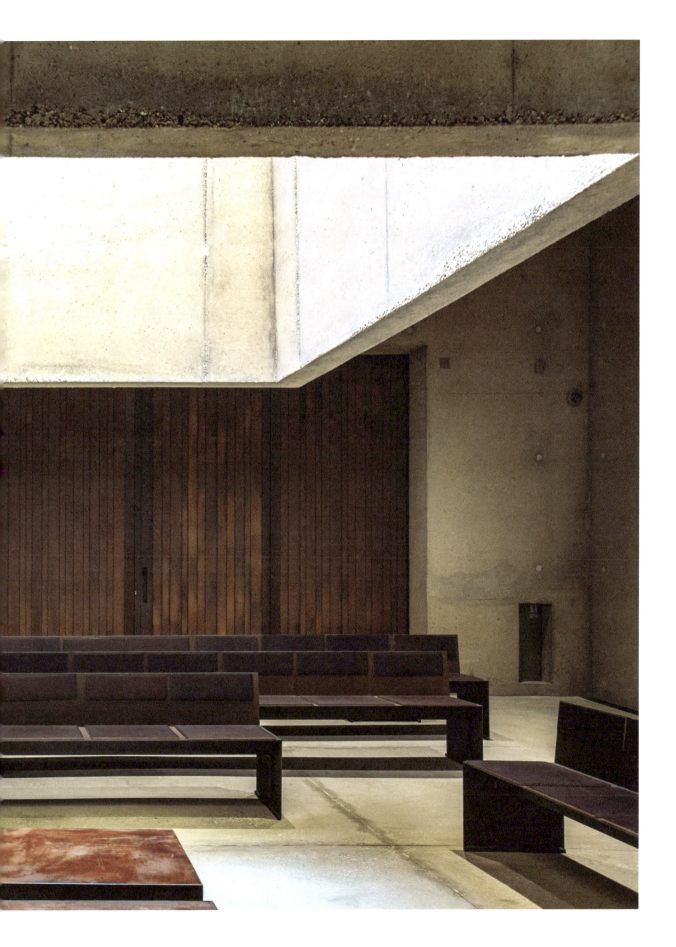

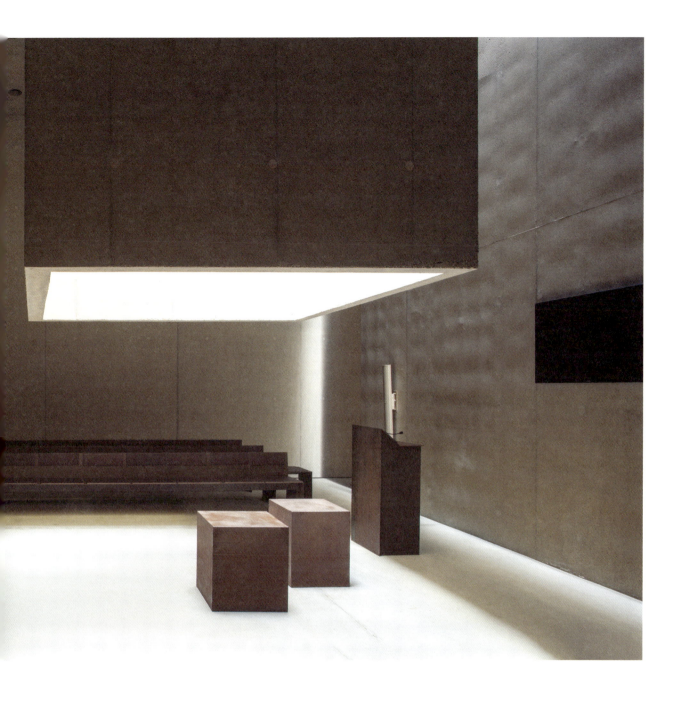

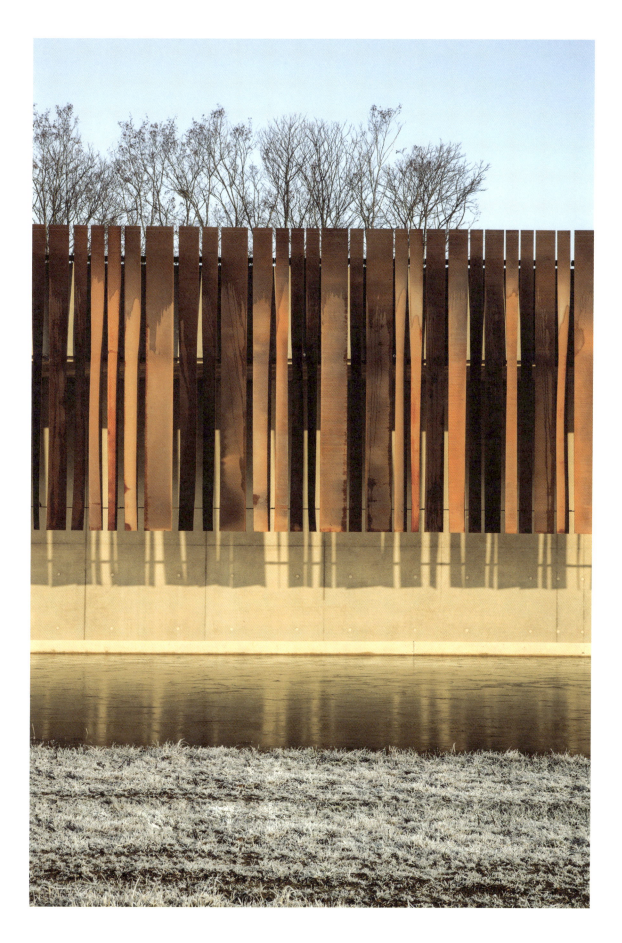

1. Main access
2. Family and visitors' entrance
3. Exit for family and visitors
4. Parking for 210 cars
5. Access for funeral service technical staff
6. Access for cafeteria service
7. Entrance to the crematorium
8. Access for the disabled people
9. Crematorium
10. Forest
11. Parking reserved for disabled
12. Wall of the forest
13. Vegetable garden
14. Columbrado - field of the urns - scattering of ash
15. Ash scattering
16. Family graves
17. Panthcon
18. Land art
19. Pedestrian and bicycle access
20. Existing vegetation
21. New vegetation
22. Swamp

Site plan

1. メイン入り口
2. 遺族、訪問者用入り口
3. 遺族、訪問者用出口
4. 駐車場（210台）
5. 従業員用入り口
6. カフェテリア通用口
7. 火葬場入り口
8. バリアフリー入り口
9. 火葬場
10. 森
11. 身障者用駐車場
12. 森林擁壁
13. 畑
14. 墓地、納棺所、散灰場
15. 散灰場
16. 家族墓
17. パンテオン
18. ランドアート
19. 歩行者、自転車用アクセス
20. 既存緑地
21. 新緑地
22. 沼地

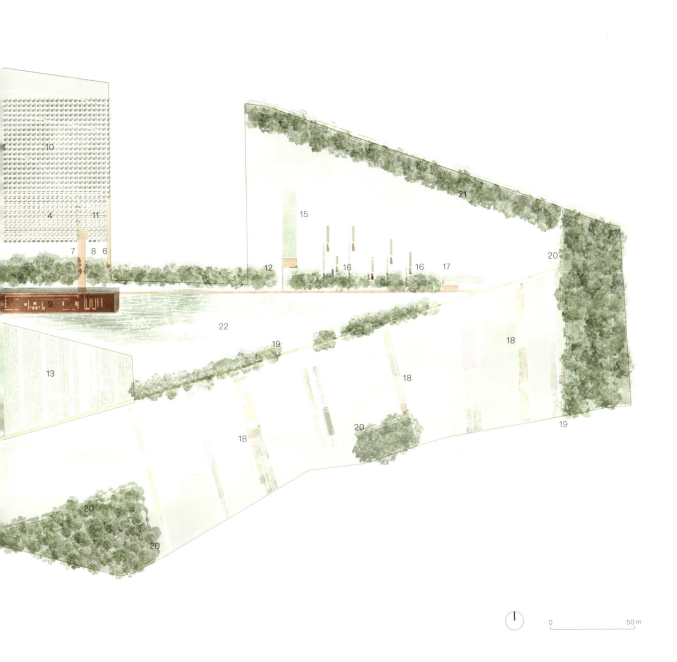

A. Access from the parking
B. Access to the crematorium
C. Access to the Columbrado - field of the urns - scattering of ash
D. Void
E. Access to the cafeteria
F. Access to the family hall
G. Access to the landscape - Scattering of ash - Columbrado - Field of the urns - Pantheon

1. Reception
2. Archive
3. Administration
4. Ladies' toilet
5. Toilet for disabled people
6. Gentlemen's toilet
7. Reception area and extensible room for the hall for 250 people
8. Room for 250 people
9. Storage
10. Transition space
11. Service stairs
12. Family room for 30 people
13. Reception area and extensible room for the hall for 75 people
14. Room
15. Waiting room and meditation space
16. Access to the area of Crematorium oven
17. Waiting room
18. Ceremony hall for receiving the urns
19. Lift
20. Control room
21. Crematorium Oven / Entrance of Coffins
22. Crematorium Oven
23. Patio
24. Cafeteria for 75 seats
25. Terrace
26. Hot meal kitchen
27. Cold meal kitchen
28. Kitchen (plates)
29. Stairs and lifts
30. Bar
31. Family room for 75 people

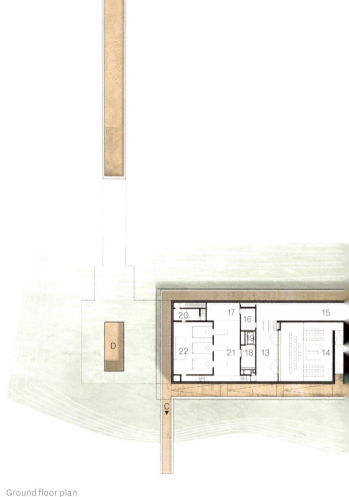

Ground floor plan

A. 駐車場側入り口
B. 火葬場入り口
C. 納骨場、納棺所、散骨場入り口
D. ヴォイド
E. カフェテリア入り口
F. 遺族、訪問者ホール入り口
G. 庭園、散骨場、納棺所、パンテオン入り口

1. 受付
2. 書庫、資料室
3. 管理室
4. 女性用トイレ
5. 身障者用トイレ

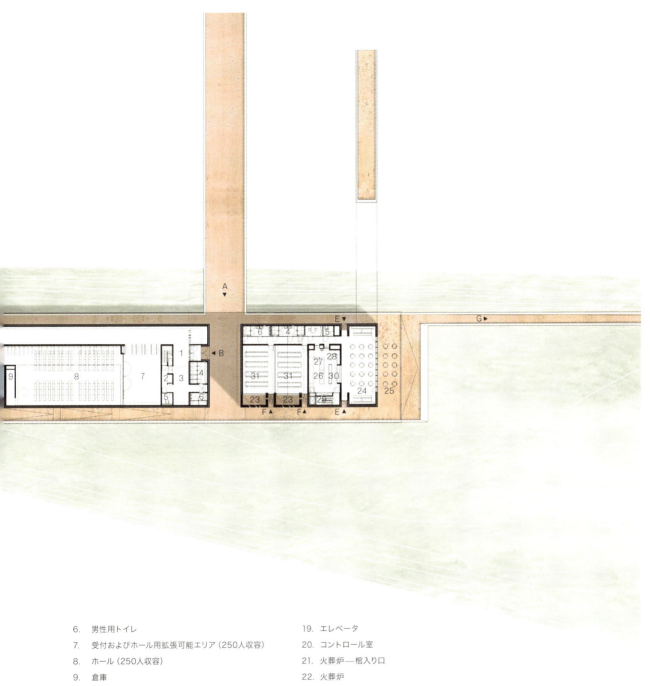

6. 男性用トイレ
7. 受付およびホール用拡張可能エリア（250人収容）
8. ホール（250人収容）
9. 倉庫
10. 前室
11. サービス用階段
12. 遺族、訪問者ホール（30人収容）
13. 受付およびホール用拡張可能エリア（75人収容）
14. ホール
15. 待合室、瞑想空間
16. 火葬炉エリア入り口
17. 待合室
18. 骨壺引き渡し、葬儀場
19. エレベータ
20. コントロール室
21. 火葬炉—棺入り口
22. 火葬炉
23. 中庭
24. カフェテリア（75席）
25. テラス
26. 調理室（加熱設備有）
27. 調理室（加熱設備無）
28. 調理室
29. 階段、エレベータ
30. バー
31. 遺族、訪問者室（75人収容）

Longitudinal section

Longitudinal section

A.	Access to the crematorium	9.	Ceremony hall for receiving the urns	18.	Refrigeration room
1.	Reception area and extensible room for the hall for 250 people	10.	Crematorium Oven / Entrance of Coffins	19.	Technical Space
2.	Administration	11.	Crematorium Oven	20.	Installation filters
3.	Ladies' toilet	12.	Family room for 75 people	21.	Hydraulic group
4.	Room for 250 people	13.	Bar	22.	Waiting room and meditation space
5.	Storage	14.	Cafeteria for 75 seats	23.	Access to the area of Crematorium oven
6.	Service stairs	15.	Terrace	24.	Waiting room for 15 people
7.	Room for 75 people	16.	Car parking for ceremony	25.	Control room
8.	Reception area and extensible room for the hall for 75 people	17.	Office	26.	Indoor charger point

168

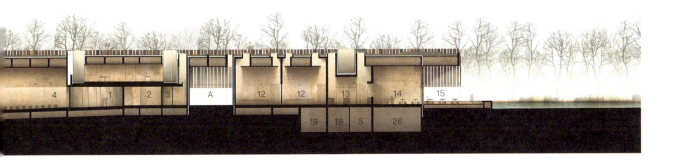

A. 火葬場入り口
1. 受付およびホール(250人収容)用拡張可能エリア
2. 管理室
3. 女性用トイレ
4. ホール(250人収容)
5. 倉庫
6. サービス用階段
7. ホール(75人収容)
8. 受付およびホール(75人収容)用拡張可能エリア
9. 骨壺引渡し、葬儀場
10. 火葬炉—棺入り口
11. 火葬炉
12. 遺族、訪問者室(75人収容)
13. バー
14. カフェテリア(75席)
15. テラス
16. 参列者用駐車場
17. オフィス
18. 冷蔵室
19. 機械室
20. 設備フィルター
21. 油圧設備
22. 待合室、瞑想空間
23. 火葬炉エリア入り口
24. 待合室(15人収容)
25. コントロール室
26. 屋内充電所

Waalse Krook Mediatheque   Gent, Belgium (2017)

Associated architects: Coussée & Goris Architecten

"Culture is a superposition of layers of history printed in the unconscious and many of them also in books that continue to happen and that brings us an encouraging human cohesion." RCR

Dematerialization

One of the most important objectives is the quest for transparent, limitless architecture, for pure space in symbiosis with nature that tends towards dematerialization.

ヴァールゼ・クローク・メディアテーク　ベルギー、ゲント（2017年）
Coussée & Goris Architectenとの共同設計

文化とは、無意識の中に、そしてつくられ続ける書物の中に印刷された歴史の層の積み重ねであり、それが私たちの望むような人間の結束を、もたらしてくれるのだ。── RCR

脱物質化

最も重要な目的のひとつは、透明で境界のない建築を希求し続けることだ。その、自然と共生する純粋な空間は、脱物質化の方向へと向かう。

A. Lammerstraat Street

B. Walpoorstraat Street

C. Grote Huideverttershoek Street

D. Korianderstraat Street

E. Kuioerskaai Street

F. Brabantdam Street

G. Korianderplein plaza

H. Green oasis on the shore

I. Main access to "New Circus"

J. Stairs between platteberg and Lammerstraat

K. New student housing building

L. New south bridge

M. Pedestrian walkway

N. Observation deck on the channel

O. Main entrance of the new library and CNM

P. Slope to Korianderplein

Q. Slope to the shore of the canal

A. Lammerstraat 通り

B. Walpoorstraat 通り

C. Grote Huideverttershoek 通り

D. Korianderstraat 通り

E. Kuioerskaai 通り

F. Brabantdam 通り

G. Korianderplein 広場

H. 水辺の緑地スペース

I. "New Circus" へのメインエントランス

J. Platteberg と Lammerstraatの間の階段

K. 新学生寮

L. 新南橋

M. 新歩行者道

N. 河川観覧デッキ

O. 新図書館とCNMへのメイン入り口

P. Korianderplein 広場へのスロープ

Q. 河川敷へのスロープ

Site plan

Ground floor

First Basement floor

1. Control
2. Security
3. Shelves for brochures
4. Digital vertical newspapers
5. Registration and reception
6. Space for return
7. Cash
8. Info PCs
9. Thematic room
10. Auto-borrowing machine
11. Newspapers and general magazines
12. Internet zone
13. Forum
14. Cafeteria
15. Storage
16. Front-office customer service
17. Public attention office
18. Information point
19. Lockers
20. Open shelves
21. Reading places
22. Classification space
23. Multimedia thesis lab. Room
24. Radio studio
25. Material tech. Radio
26. Live music
27. Space for live music management
28. Proximity office
29. Collection focused on youth
30. Stories-telling corner
31. Workplaces
32. Places for school work
33. Youth forum
34. Youth workshop
35. Bike parking
36. Reservations
37. Agora
38. Cubus

Fourth floor

Third floor

Second floor

First floor

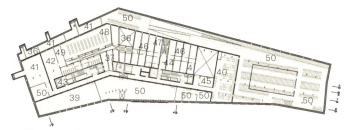
Second basement floor

1.	管理室	36.	予約
2.	セキュリティ	37.	アゴラ
3.	チラシ等スタンド	38.	クブス
4.	デジタル新聞閲覧室	39.	分別所
5.	登録カウンター	40.	倉庫、更衣室
6.	返却スペース	41.	機械室
7.	支払い	42.	清掃
8.	情報用端末	43.	更衣室
9.	テーマ室	44.	実験ラボ
10.	自動貸出機	45.	技術ワークショップ
11.	新聞、一般雑誌閲覧室	46.	カウンター
12.	インターネット	47.	ミラーウォール
13.	フォーラム	48.	ユース図書室
14.	カフェテリア	49.	一般用クローク
15.	倉庫	50.	共有会議室
16.	一般窓口	51.	マッターリンクキャビネット
17.	窓口	52.	文化アゴラ
18.	情報窓口	53.	自動貸出機
19.	ロッカー	54.	文化専門コレクション
20.	開架書庫	55.	文化フォーラム
21.	閲覧室	56.	文化ワークショップ
22.	分別所	57.	学生用閲覧室
23.	マルチメディア論文ラボ	58.	知識のアゴラ
24.	ラジオスタジオ	59.	情報専門書架
25.	ラジオ機材室	60.	古書庫
26.	ライブ音楽	61.	実験庭園
27.	ライブ音楽企画室	62.	知識ワークショップ
28.	オフィス	63.	メディアセンター
29.	ユース向け図書	64.	閲覧室
30.	読み聞かせコーナー	65.	作業室
31.	作業場	66.	オフィス
32.	学校作業室	67.	勉強室
33.	ユースフォーラム	68.	相談窓口
34.	ユースワークショップ		
35.	駐輪場		

39.	Classification space	49.	Public cloakroom
40.	Storage-Changing room	50.	Common meeting rooms
41.	Technical rooms	51.	Cabinet matter link
42.	Cleaning	52.	Agora of culture
43.	Changing rooms	53.	Self-borrowing counters
44.	Experimentation lab.	54.	Culture Collection
45.	Technical workshop	55.	Forum of culture
46.	Counter	56.	Culture workshop
47.	Mirror wall	57.	Organization to support studies
48.	Youth library	58.	Agora of knowledge
		59.	Collection focused on knowledge
		60.	Library of hereditary assets
		61.	Knowledge forum
		62.	Knowledge workshop
		63.	Media center
		64.	Reading places
		65.	Working rooms
		66.	Offices
		67.	Study room
		68.	Consultation room

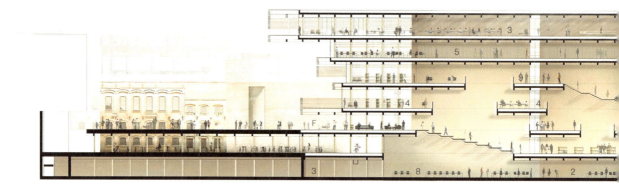

Longitudinal section

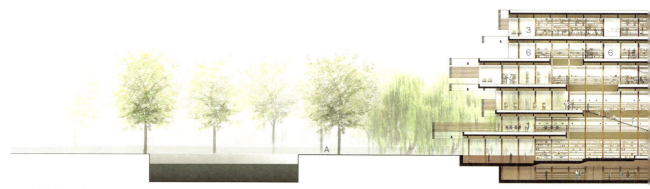

Longitudinal section

A. Green oasis on the shore
B. Slope for bicycles
C. New student housing building
D. Pedestrian walkway
E. Observation deck on the channel
F. Main entrance of the new library and CNM

1. Thematic room
2. Agora
3. Space for books classification
4. Reading room
5. Storage
6. Working cell
7. Lockers
8. Experimentation Lab.
9. Agora of knowledge
10. Cafeteria

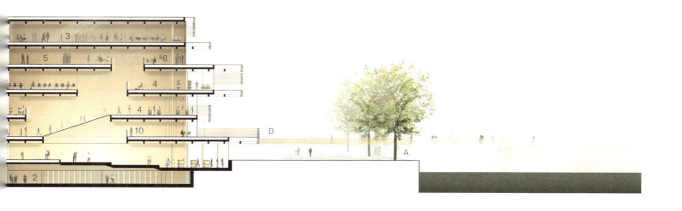

A. 水辺の緑地スペース
B. 自転車用スロープ
C. 新学生寮
D. 歩行者道
E. 河川観覧デッキ
F. 新図書館とCNMへのメイン入り口

1. テーマ室
2. アゴラ
3. 図書分類室
4. 読書室
5. 倉庫
6. 作業スペース
7. ロッカー
8. 実験室
9. 知識のアゴラ
10. カフェテリア

La Vila

Geography of Dreams

Actual project information
プロジェクトの最新状況

LA VILA   RCR LAB·A   Site
42°12'33"N 2°25'20"E

ラ・ヴィラ   RCR LAB·A   敷地

2. RCR Arquitectes

Creative Architecture Studio born the year 1988 in Olot of the hand of Rafael Aranda, Carme Pigem and Ramon Vilalta.

RCRアーキテクツ
1988にオロットの地でラファエル・アランダ、カルマ・ピジェム、ラモン・ヴィラルタによって設立された建築創造ワークショップ。

3. RCR Bunka

Foundation created by RCR Arquitectes to stimulate socially the assessment of architecture and landscape, and, implicitly, arts and culture in general.

RCR Bunka
建築とランドスケープ、芸術と文化全体の社会的な価値に対する認識を向上させるべくRCRアーキテクツによって設立された財団。

2. Barberí space
RCR Studio
バルベリ・スペース
RCRスタジオ

1. La Vila
RCR Laboratory
ラ・ヴィラ
RCRラボラトリー

3. Bunka Space
RCR Archive
ブンカ・スペース
RCRアーカイヴ

1. RCR Lab·A

Open architecture laboratory space to develop creative research and transversality.

RCR Lab·A
リサーチや創造の横断性に対する開発のために開かれた建築研究施設。

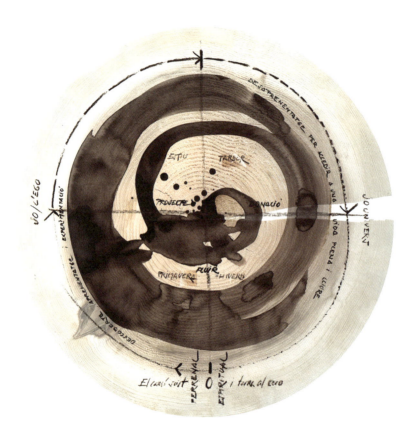

DREAM

What we want to show here, is the dream that drives us,the story we have started to write, and that we would like to share with you from the outset although it has still to be shaped.

Nature, written in capital letters, is and has been an inexhaustible source of inspiration both personally and architecturally. La Vila, a place populated by forest, water and memory, with which we had a first explore the creation of an open laboratory.

A laboratory that can change people's awareness of perception and that inspires the emergence of new relationships and behaviours. Beyond its intrinsic complexity, we would like the laboratory to be transversal, comprehensive and built in the most essential and genuine way possible.

To become a place of worldwide reference, from an almost hidden enclave. For what is being done here, for what happens here, for those who come here, for the magic released here — in short, for the creativity that is generated here: a shadow moving through the fog.

夢

ここで私たちが示そうとしているのは、私たちを突き動かしている夢、私たちが書きはじめた物語、私たちがこれを読んでいるあなたと一から共有したいと思っている、未だかたちづくられていないもの、についてである。

大文字の自然は、個人にとっても建築にとっても無尽蔵にインスピレーションを与えてくれる源泉である。ラ・ヴィラは広く深い森、水、そして記憶が蓄積されている場所であり、私たちは2002年にそこに建つ家屋と池の改修プロジェクトを手がけたことがきっかけでその土地と巡り合い、現在は、そこに創造のための開かれた研究施設をつくろうとしている。

その研究施設の目的は、人びとの知覚に対する意識を変容させ、新しい関係性とふるまいを促すことである。それ自体が抱えている複雑さのさらに先にある、横断的で総合的、そして可能な限り最も本質的で純粋な、そういう施設になることを願っている。

それはほとんど隠されたような辺境の場所から世界につながる、後世の人たちにとっての参照となるだろう。そこで何かを起こす人のために、そこで起こっていることのために、そこを訪れる人びとのために、そこで起こる魔法のために、つまり霧の中を動く影のように、そこで生まれる創造性のために。

La Vila

Landscape

Field and forest

Walls

Torrent de Can Bosch

Water

La Vila is now rich in shades, like a well-drawn geography, like a great book open for the central page. So much done until here, so much remains to be done.

Our actions depend on the assessment and understanding of what has been bequeathed to us. So now you must look, feel, smell … and open the whole body so that it is receptive to all its ample wonder.

水

ラ・ヴィラには豊かな色彩の広がりがある。それは精密に描かれた地図のようでもあり、真ん中で開かれた大きな書物のようでもある。ここでこれまでに多くのことが生成され、これからも多くのものが生まれるだろう。

私たちに与えられたこの存在を評価し理解することは、私たちがこれから行うべき行動に深く関わっている。今成すべきことは、見ること、触れること、匂いを確かめること……身体のすべてを開いてこの場所の素晴らしさのすべてを知覚することである。

218

Torrent de Batllia

Casa Pairal La Vila and Bassa de La Vila

Casa Pairal La Vila and Cabana

Casa Pairal La Vila

Casa Pairal La Vila

Bassa de La Vila, RCR Arquitectes 2002

Casa Pairal La Vila and Cabana

Can Capsec, Cabana and Era

L'Era

La Vila

"Deepening in our common human nature, we can achieve something extraordinary, integral. That is why the most extraordinary comes from the experience of one's daily life." RCR

私たちが共通してもっている人間らしさを深めることで、特別で総体的な何かを実現することができる。だから、もっとも特別なことは、日常生活の経験からくるのである。
— RCR

Reseach and studies about the place　　この場所についてのリサーチとスタディ

Meteorological data   気候データ

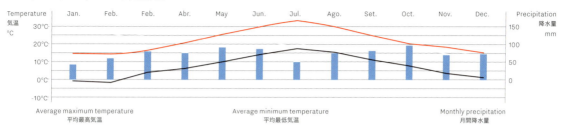

Summary of meteorological data	
Absolute maximum temperature	40.4 °C (5/7/2015)
Absolute minimum temperature	-7 °C (5/2/2015)
Average monthly precipitation	70 mm
Total monthly precipitation	840 mm
Relative humidity average	72 %
Global average of daily solar radiation	75.2 MJ/m²

気候データの概要	
絶対最高気温	40.4 °C (5/7/2015)
絶対最低気温	-7 °C (5/2/2015)
平均月間降水量	70 mm
月間合計降水量	840 mm
平均相対湿度	72 %
1日あたりの総合平均日射量	75.2 MJ/m²

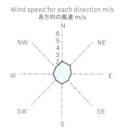

Average speed of dominant winds of South-West 1.3 m/s
風の平均方向 / 速度：南西1.3 m/s

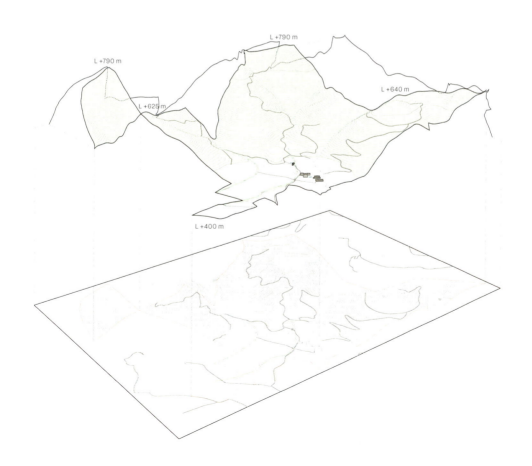

245

"If you are not used to looking at the sky, the stars... or you do not allow yourself to become enchanted. If you are not used to touching the earth, the trees... or drinking water that bubbles up from natural springs. If you are not used to listening to the sounds of the air... or the scent of the wind. If you do not glimpse the beauty in nature at every step you take and you do not want to discover its mystery or to love it. Then it is unlikely that you will be able to comprehend many of our feelings, thoughts and attitudes, or glimpse the strength and energy that nature gives us!" RCR

もしもあなたが普段から空や星を見ることに慣れていないなら、またはあなたがそれらを見て感動を覚えることがないのなら……。もしもあなたが大地や木々に手で触れたり、自然の泉から湧き出る水を飲むことに慣れていないのなら……。もしもあなたが空気の音を聞いたり風の匂いを嗅ぐことに慣れていないのなら……。もしも自然の中で一歩足を進める度にその美しさに見惚れることがなく、そして自然の謎を見つけたり、それらを愛すこともないのなら、おそらくあなたは私たちの気持ちや思考、態度の多くを理解することも、そして自然が私たちに与えてくれる力とエネルギーを見ることもできないだろう。── RCR

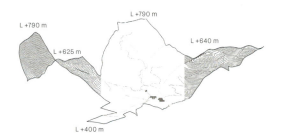

Topography
地形
1,358,000 m²

Hydrology
河川
18,650 m²

1,4 %

Paths
道
18,200 m²

1,3 %

Existing buildings
既存建物
2,118 m² (occupation)

0,16 %

Vegetation
植栽
Forest: 1,114,700 m²
Fields: 243,300 m²

18 %   82 %

Type of crop
農業用地
243,300 m²
Grassland, prairie, irrigation, forest
芝生、牧草地、灌漑用地、森林

2 % 6 % 7 %   85 %

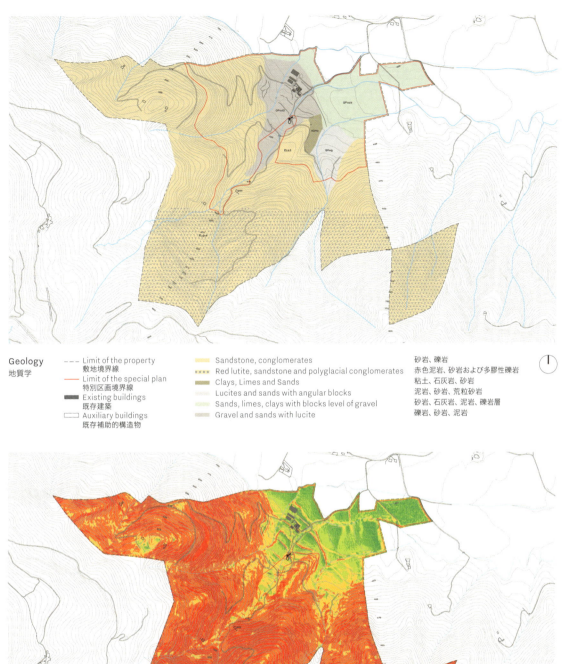

Geology
地質学

- - - Limit of the property
敷地境界線
— Limit of the special plan
特別区画境界線
■ Existing buildings
既存建築
□ Auxiliary buildings
既存補助的構造物

▨ Sandstone, conglomerates — 砂岩、礫岩
▧ Red lutite, sandstone and polyglacial conglomerates — 赤色泥岩、砂岩および多膠性礫岩
▨ Clays, Limes and Sands — 粘土、石灰岩、砂岩
▨ Lucites and sands with angular blocks — 泥岩、砂岩、荒粒砂岩
▨ Sands, limes, clays with blocks level of gravel — 砂岩、石灰岩、泥岩、礫岩層
▨ Gravel and sands with lucite — 礫岩、砂岩、泥岩

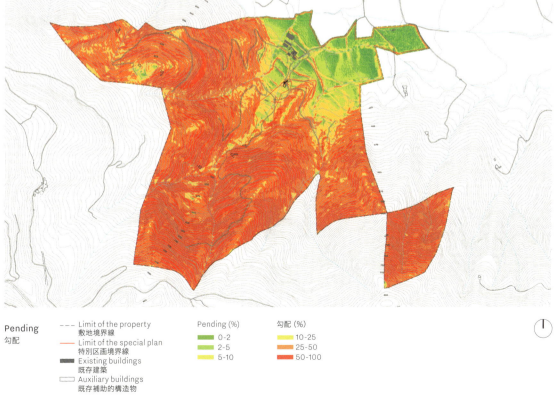

Pending
勾配

- - - Limit of the property
敷地境界線
— Limit of the special plan
特別区画境界線
■ Existing buildings
既存建築
□ Auxiliary buildings
既存補助的構造物

Pending (%) / 勾配 (%)
- 0-2
- 2-5
- 5-10
- 10-25
- 25-50
- 50-100

"Life, like water. The closer to the source,
  the greater the clarity with which we can live.
The complexity of life can be like a clear or
  a muddy pool.
Lived in serenity, stillness and essentiality,
  life is crystal clear.
Lived in excessive movement, it is murky
  and muddy." RCR

人生は、まるで水のようだ。私たちの人生も、その根源に近
づくほど透明度が増す。
人生の複雑さは、透明な水のようにも、あるいは泥水のよ
うにもなりうるものだ。
静けさと確かさ、そして本質の中に生きるなら、人生はガラ
スのように透明になる。
そして過度の動きの中に生きるなら、それは暗い泥のように
なる。— RCR

Birds of this place　　　この地に生息する鳥類

PASSERIFORMES　スズメ目
PÀRIDS　シジュウカラ科

MALLARENGA D'AIGUA
PARUS PALUSTRIS
ハシブトガラ

MALLARENGA EMPLOMALLADA
PARUS CRISTATUS
カンムリガラ

MALLARENGA BLAVA
PARUS CAERULEUS
アオガラ

MALLARENGA PETITA
PARUS ATER
ヒガラ

MALLARENGA CARBONERA
PARUS MAJOR
シジュウカラ

EGITALIDS　エナガ科

MALLARENGA CUALLARGA
AEGITHALOS CAUDATUS
エナガ

FRINGÍL·LIDS　アトリ科

CADERNERA
CARDUELIS CARDUELIS
ゴシキヒワ

GAIG
GARRULUS GLANDARIUS
カケス

SÍTITS　ゴジュウカラ科

PICA-SOQUES BLAU
SITTA EUROPAEA
ゴジュウカラ

CORACIFORMES　ブッポウソウ目
ALCEDÍNIDS　カワセミ科

BLAUET
ALCEDO ATTHIS
カワセミ

UPUPIDS　ヤツガシラ科

PUPUT
UPUPA EPOPS
ヤツガシラ

PÍCIFORMES　キツツキ目
PÍCIDS　キツツキ科

COLLTORT
JYNX TORQUILLA
アリスイ

PICOT GRASER GROS
DENDROCOPOS MAJOR
アカゲラ

ESTRIGIFORMES　フクロウ目
ESTRÍGIDS　フクロウ科

DUC
DUBO DUBO
ワシミミズク

CARADRIFORMES　チドリ目
ESCOLOPÀCIDS　シギ科

BECADA
SCOLOPAX RUSTICOLA
ヤマシギ

LÀNIDS　モズ科

ESCORXADOR
LANIUS COLLURIO
セアカモズ

SCOLOPACIDAE　シギ科

POLIT CANTAIRE
NUMENIUS PHAEOPUS
チュウシャクシギ

CORACIFORMES　ブッポウソウ目
MEROPIDS　ハチクイ科

ABELLEROL
MEROPS APIASTER
ヨーロッパハチクイ

GRÜIFORMES　ツル目
RÀL·LIDS　クイナ科

POLLA D'AIGUA
GALLINULA CHLOROPUS
バン

FALCONIFORMES　ハヤブサ下目
FALCÒNIDS　タカ科

ESPARVER VULGAR
ACCIPITER NISUS
ハイタカ

ÀGUILA MARCENCA
CIRCAETUS GALLICUS
チョウヒワシ

FALCÓ MOSTATXUT
FALCO SUBBUTEO
チゴハヤブサ

ACCIPÍTRIDS　タカ科

ASTOR
ACCIPITER GENTILIS
オオタカ

CICONIFORMES　コウノトリ目
ARDÈIDS　サギ科

BERNAT PESCAIRE
ARDEA CINEREA
アオサギ

Animals of this place   この地に生息する動物

INSECTÍVORS 食虫動物
SORICIDAE トガリネズミ科   TALPIDAE モグラ科   ERINACEIDAE ハリネズミ科   SCIURIDAE リス科

MUSARANYA COMUNA
CROCIDURA RUSSULA
ヨーロッパジネズミ

TALP
TALPA EUROPAEA
ヨーロッパモグラ

ERIÇÓ COMÚ
ERINACEUS EUROPAEUS
ヨーロッパハリネズミ

ESQUIROL
SCIURUS VULGARIS
リス

QUIRÒPTERS コウモリ類
VESPERTILIONIDAE ヒナコウモリ科   RHINOLOPHIDAE キクガシラコウモリ科

RAT-PENAT DE BOSC
BARBASTELLA BARBASTELLUS
ヨーロッパチブコウモリ

RAT-PENAT NÒCTUL PETIT
NYCTALUS LEISLERI
ユーラシアコヤマコウモリ

RAT-PENAT DE FERRADURA MEDITERRANI
RHINOLOPHUS EURYALE
キクガシラコウモリ

RAT-PENAT DE FERRADURA PETIT
RHINOLOPHUS HIPPOSIDEROS
ヒメキクガシラコウモリ

ROSEGADORS ネズミ類
MURIDAE ネズミ科

RATOLÍ DE BOSC
APODEMUS SYLVATICUS
モリアカネズミ

RATA NEGRA
RATTUS RATTUS
クマネズミ

RATOLÍ DOMÈSTIC
MUS MUSCULUS
ハツカネズミ

RATA TOPINERA COMUNA
MICROTUS DUODECIMOCOSTATUS
ハタネズミ

CARNÍVORS 肉食動物
MUSTELIDAE イタチ科

TURÓ
MUSTELA PUTORIUS
ヨーロッパケナガイタチ

GORJABLANC
MARTES FOINA
ムナジロテン

MARTA
MARTES MARTES
マツテン

TEIXÓ
MELES MELES
ヨーロッパアナグマ

CÀNIDS イヌ科   VIVERRIDAE ジャコウネコ科   FELIDAE ネコ科

GUILLA
VULPES VULPES
アカギツネ

LLOP
CANIS LUPUS
タイリクオオカミ

GAT MESQUER
GENETTA GENETTA
ヨーロッパジェネット

GAT SALVATGE
FELIS SILVESTRIS
ヤマネコ

LAGOMORFS ウサギ目
LEPORIDAE ウサギ科   ARTIODÀCTILS 偶蹄類
                                 SUIDAE イノシシ科   CERVIDAE シカ科

CONILL
ORYCTOLAGUS CUNICULUS
アナウサギ

LLEBRE
LEPUS EUROPAEUS
ヤブノウサギ

PORC SENGLAR
SUS SCROFA
イノシシ

CÉRVOL
CERVUS ELAPHUS
アカシカ

Relevant buildings of this area　　　このエリアの関連する建物群

1. Església de Sant Andreu del Coll
サン・アンドレウ・デル・コル教会

2. Església de Sant Miquel del Coll
サン・ミケル・デル・コル教会

3. Església de Santa Margarida de Bianya
サンタ・マルガリーダ・デ・ビアーニャ教会

4. Església de Sant Pere Despuig
サン・ペラ・デスプッチ教会

5. La Vila　ラ・ヴィラ

6. Molí de la Vila
ラ・ヴィラの水車小屋

7. Mas La Torre
マス・ラ・トーレ邸

8. Mas Les Aulines
ラス・アウリーナス邸

9. Mas Bossa de dalt
ボッサ・ダ・ダルト邸

10. Masia del Llac
湖畔の邸宅

11. Bassa de la Vila
ラ・ヴィラの貯水池

12. Casa Horitzó
カサ・ホリゾンテ

261

"NUVOLINA, a fabulated synthesis that mixes longings and experiences, intuitions, dreams... and above all, the inspiring impulse of La Vila, with the discovery of its fog, the water, the forest, the vegetation, the ruins, spaces, books, history, stories... A place that is meaningful with a latent spirit." RCR

ヌヴォリーナは、憧れと経験、直感と夢などの混合物である。何よりここには、私たちをラ・ヴィラのプロジェクトへと突き動かしたインスピレーションの源である、霧、水、森、植物、遺跡、宇宙、本などがある。潜在意識にとって意義深い場所。── RCR

Site plan drawn in 18th century
18世紀に描かれたラ・ヴィラ周辺の地図

History

La Vila has layers of history, nature, documents and architecture. There must be carried out archaeology to bring to light traces of a written and erased past. And in the exfoliation process to distinguish which layers, which leaves, stand out and remain visible. Water, fountains, fog and dew. Life and its manifestations, with forests and animals, crops and orchards, people… footprint on footprint. The stones sculpted by time and hands.

歴史

ラ・ヴィラには自然、文書、建築という歴史の層がある。そこで過去に記され、あるいは消されたものの痕跡に光を当てるべく、考古学的な作業を行う必要があるだろう。それらの層や文書を一枚一枚剥離させながら理解を深めていく作業において、さまざまなものが明らかにされていく。水、泉、霧そして露。それらが生きていた証、森、動物、灌漑、畑、人びと……足跡の上に重ねられたさらなる足跡たち。石は時間の経過によって、または人の手によって、削り取られていった。

Library of La Vila
ラ・ヴィラの蔵書棚

Document of consecration Pope Pius XII
ローマ教皇ピウス十二世による聖別文書

"When understanding emerges from a specific discipline, from itself, no matter how deep, it is always a biased, partial view that hinders our establishment and/or our relations with the whole." RCR

その理解が、あるひとつの分野だけのなかから導き出されたものならば、それはどんなに深かったとしても、偏って部分的な理解に過ぎないため、全体と私たちの関係を構築することを妨げるのだ。 — RCR

Furniture and objects　　　　家具と小物類

Toilet seat / Wood	Cradle / Wood	Chair / Wood	Mixing box / Wood	Table / Wood	Cabinet / Wood
便座 / 木	ゆりかご / 木	椅子 / 木	こね機 / 木	テーブル / 木	キャビネット / 木
53 x 56 x 90 cm	98 x 69 x 68 cm	40 x 44 x 100 cm	152 x 65.5 x 124 cm	Ø 147 cm	167 x 64 x 247 cm

Cradle / Wood	Dressing table / Wood, marble, glass	Washing basin / Wood, marble, glass	Rocking chair / Wood	Drawers / Wood, marble	Mirror / Wood, glass
ゆりかご / 木	鏡台 / 木、大理石、ガラス	手洗い台 / 木、大理石、ガラス	ゆり椅子 / 木	引き出し / 木、大理石	鏡 / 木、ガラス
115 x 40 x 102 cm	80 x 56.3 x 150 cm	50 x 53 x 132 cm	52.5 x 80 x 110 cm	112 x 86.5 x 58 cm	107 x 5 x 87 cm

Trunk / Wood, metal	Table / Wood	Chair / Wood, esparto	Chair / Wood, metal, leather	Storage / Wood, marble	Cabinet / Wood
トランク / 木、金属	テーブル / 木	椅子 / 木、藁	椅子 / 木、金属、革	物入れ / 木、大理石	キャビネット / 木
77 x 52 x 50 cm	231 x 113 x 82 cm	41 x 40 x 88 cm	70 x 60 x 108 cm	142 x 53 x 51 cm	62 x 120 x 284 cm

Bench / Wood	Chair / Wood, esparto	Bench / Wood, esparto	Rocking chair / Wood, esparto	Drawers / Wood, marble	Cabinet / Wood, glass
ベンチ / 木	椅子 / 木、藁	ベンチ / 木、藁	ゆり椅子 / 木、藁	引き出し / 木、大理石	キャビネット / 木、ガラス
187 x 67 x 104 cm	41 x 40 x 88 cm	274 x 50 x 86 cm	60 x 72 x 110 cm	116 x 61 x 114 cm	132 x 63 x 249 cm

Chair / Wood, metal, leather	Chair / Wood, metal, leather	Small table / Wood	Bench / Wood	Recliner / Wood, esparto	Recliner / Wood
椅子 / 木、金属、革	椅子 / 木、金属、革	小机 / 木	ベンチ / 木、藁	背もたれ椅子 / 木、藁	背もたれ椅子 / 木
69.5 x 57 x 100 cm	70 x 60 x 104 cm	55 x 30 x 45 cm	111.5 x 43.5 x 82 cm	43.5 x 34 x 85 cm	42 x 44 x 85 cm

Drawers / Wood	Olot drawing / Wood	Bed / Wood	Bedside table / Wood, marble	Bedside table / Wood, marble	Book shelves / Wood, glass
引き出し / 木	オロット画 / 木	ベッド / 木	寝具脇机 / 木、大理石	寝具脇机 / 木、大理石	書物棚 / 木、ガラス
110 x 44 x 101 cm	61 x 1 x 51.5 cm	140 x 188 x 220 cm	41.5 x 39 x 91 cm	46 x 43 x 100 cm	156 x 41 x 200 cm

Desk / Wood	Table / Wood, marble	Desk / Wood	La Vila and Les Moles Farm plan map / Wood, paper, glass	Pujolas and Cambra Fosca Farm plan map / Wood, paper, glass	Bed / Wood
机 / 木	テーブル / 木、大理石	机 / 木	ラ・ヴィラ、ラス・モラス農地計画図 / 木、紙、ガラス	プジョラス、カンブラ・フォスカ農地計画図 / 木、紙、ガラス	ベッド / 木
121 x 46 x 148 cm	154 x 56 x 94 cm	100 x 91 x 81 cm	90 x 3 x 76 cm	98 x 3 x 77 cm	220 x 165 x 155 cm

Balance
秤
51 x 23 x 15 cm

Coffee glinder
珈琲豆粉砕機
19 x 17 x 22 cm

Coffee glinder
珈琲豆粉砕機
13.5 x 13.5 x 21 cm

Baking pan
焼鍋
Ø 22 cm L 23 cm

Bucket
手桶
Ø 14 cm L 35 cm

Pot
鍋
44 x 18 x 16 cm

Buzzer
ベル
Ø 8 cm

Vase
水瓶
Ø 15 cm

Pot
鍋
Ø 35 cm

Pot
鍋
Ø 52 cm

Table
テーブル
80 x 235 x 77 cm

Chair
椅子
42 x 47 x 89 cm

Grill
グリル
11 x 31 cm

Tray
トレー
Ø 42 cm

Pot
鍋
Ø 24 cm

Vase
水瓶
Ø 20 cm

Pot
鍋
Ø 23.5 cm

Chair
椅子
44 x 41 x 89 cm

Bench
ベンチ
144 x 25 x 46 cm

Economic kitchen
省エネルギー型調理用炉
63 x 45 x 62 cm

Stove
ストーヴ
40 x 56 x 67 cm

Wine boot and stand
ワインブートとスタンド
41 x 64 x 75 cm

Table
テーブル
170 x 77 x 78 cm

Pitchers' bench
水差し用台座
120 x 42 x 61 cm

Candle stand
蝋燭立
10 x 10 x 14.5 cm

Oil lamp
オイルランプ
Ø 9 cm x 15 cm

Oil lamp
オイルランプ
Ø 8.5 cm x 17 cm

Bowl
椀
Ø 11.5 cm x 8 cm

Oil lamp
オイルランプ
9.5 x 6 x 19.5 cm

Oil lamp
オイルランプ
16 x 16 x 49 cm

Pot
鍋
29 x 25 x 29 cm

Pot
鍋
24 x 20 x 21 cm

Pot
鍋
27 x 23 x 20 cm

Sewing machine
ミシン
37 x 19 x 29 cm

Sewing machine box
ミシン箱
51 x 23.5 x 30 cm

Sewing machine with table
ミシンとミシン台
84 x 45 x 75 cm

Lump
ランプ
15 x 11 x 24 cm

Broom
箒
85 cm

Broom
箒
58 cm

Balance
秤
27 x 34 x 48 cm

Pot
鍋
33 x 27 x 23 cm

Cup board
食器棚
70 x 48 x 189 cm

271

"We strive to find the clearest possible synthesis to explain the intuitions, sensations, emotions and thoughts that we experience and accompany us in the course of the process."
RCR

私たちは、そのプロセスの過程で私たちが体験し、私たちに伴った直感、感覚、感情、そして思考というものを説明するために、できるだけクリアで統合的なものを見出そうと努力している。 ── RCR

Existing buildings
Casa Pairal La Vila

既存建築
カサ・パイラル・ラ・ヴィラ邸

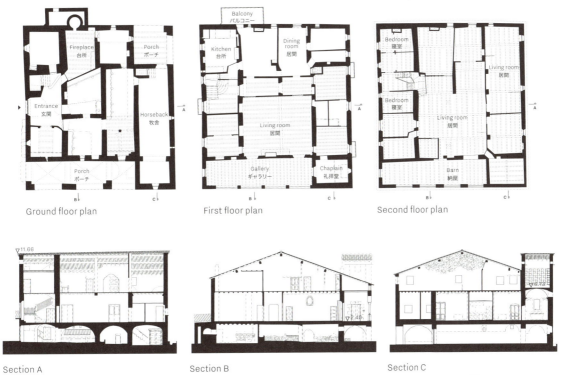

Ground floor plan

First floor plan

Second floor plan

Section A

Section B

Section C

277

Existing buildings
Can Capsec

既存建築
カン・カップセック邸

First floor plan

Ground floor plan

South-east elevation

North-west elevation

Section B

South-west elevation

North-east elevation

Section A

Existing buildings
Cabana i Era

既存建築
小屋と脱穀場

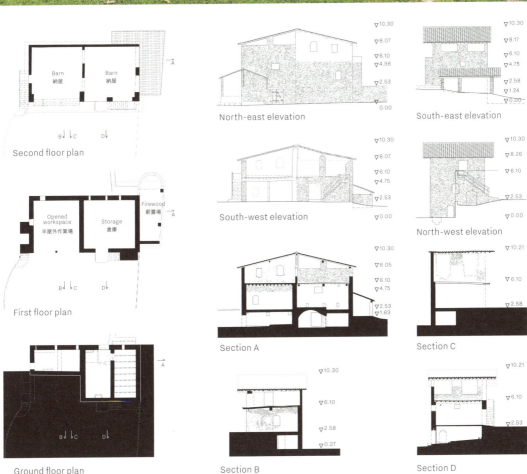

"The same words can take on different meanings in the course of life, but there is a huge leap towards understanding, towards its meaning, when its contents is truly experienced. Only then can they be erased forever." RCR

同じ言葉が、人生の過程において異なる意味をもつようになることがある。けれどもそれが経験を伴ったとき、そこにはその意味へと向かう、その言葉の理解への大きな飛躍がある。その時に初めて、その言葉を永久に忘れることができるのだ。— RCR

Existing buildings
Bassa de La Vila   RCR Arquitectes. 2002

既存建築
ラ・ヴィラの貯水池   RCRアーキテクツ設計　2002年

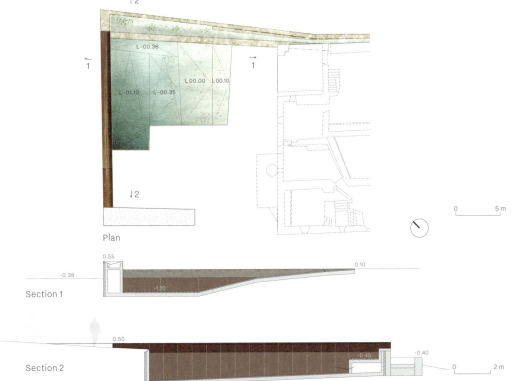

Plan

Section 1

Section 2

Existing buildings
Magatzems i Estable

既存建築
倉庫と牧舎

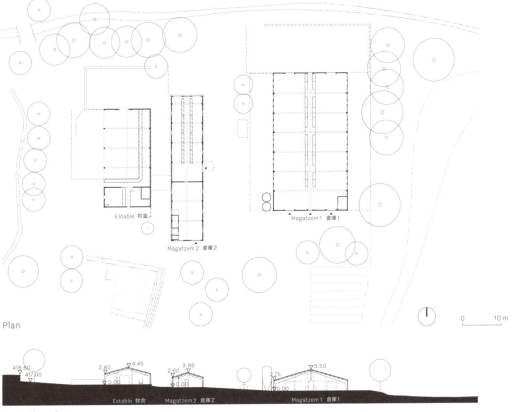

Plan

General section

"Architecture is, above all, an act of generosity. Architects create things for men and they offer them all of the areas where they develop their lives. They want them to find the environment necessary to achieve the greatest dream: feeling that you are understood in a natural and social context." RCR

建築とはまず何よりも、寛大な行為なのである。
建築家は人間のために何かをつくり、そして人がそこで生活を展開していくためのあらゆる場所を提供する。建築家は、人間の最も大きな夢——自然と社会の文脈のなかで自分が理解されていると感じること——を成し遂げるために必要な環境を、人びとがその建築の中に見出してほしいと願うのだ。—— RCR

Existing buildings
Molí de La Vila i Cabana

既存建築
ラ・ヴィラの水車と小屋

Molí de La Vila　　ラ・ヴィラの水車

Cabana　　小屋

First floor plan

Second floor plan

Ground floor plan

0　　　　5 m

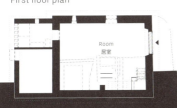

First floor plan

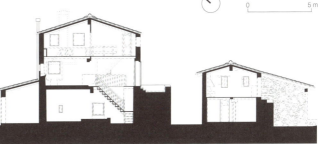

Section

Ground floor plan

Global proposal in progress　　　　進行中のグローバルプロポーザル

"Life as such has no meaning. Its meaning is created on a journey that we have to fill with content and significance that make it closer and more satisfactory for us. There is always a choice, a dream, at the source of this journey—what we want it to be and is not yet—and we shape ourselves while we are walking. We are not tourists because we look and we want to see, because we listen and we want to understand, because we want to delve deeper and not slip on the surface, because we want to be thrilled and not wander along like spectators.

Sharing this journey means discussing, feeling relieved and not indispensable, feeling enriched as a group, feeling the presence of the whole and a sense of belonging, relegating individual reason, and raising our shared creativity to levels of excellence that we cannot reach as individuals.

Creativity is broad and open. It is timeless and varied. In our case, the initiative has to do with architecture, landscape, design, publishing, photography, research and so on. The architecture with a spirit that we seek is born from the vital intensity of the materialisation of our dreams on a long-distance journey. Because in our case, life and architecture are not separate entities. They merge in plenitude, accompanied by the conviction that we are all universe and, evolved, we will always be able to remain together." RCR

人生そのものには意味などない。人生の意味というのは、その旅路の途中において、それぞれが自分の満足のゆくやり方で、その内容と意義をつくり出していくものなのだ。その旅のはじめには常に選択肢があり、夢がある。それは私たちがそうなりたいと願うもの、そしてまだそうなれていない何か。そういうものを、私たちはその道を歩きながらかたちづくっていく。その道の上で、私たちは観光客なのではない。私たちは、注意深く見つめ、そしてもっとよく見たいと思っている。私たちは注意深く耳を傾け、理解したいと思う。その表面を滑るのではなく、深く掘り込んでいきたいと願う。観客としてさまよい歩くのではなく、当事者としてスリルを味わいたいのである。

この旅を誰かと共有するということは、議論することであり、自分が必要不可欠な存在であるというよりはそこに居ることへのやすらぎを感じることであり、集団としての充実を感じることであり、全体の存在と、そこに属しているという感覚を得ることであり、個人のエゴをつらぬくのではなく、個人では到達することのできないような卓越したレベルに達するべく、共有された創造性を高めることである。

創造性は広く、開かれたものである。それは時を超え、変化していく。私たちの場合には、それは建築やランドスケープ、デザインや書籍、写真や研究をつくり、行うための原動力となる。私たちが求める精神によってつくられる建築は、この長い旅路の中で生まれる夢を物質化するために、強い生命力をもって生まれる。なぜなら、私たちにとって、人生と建築は分け隔てるものができないものなのだから。それは、私たちが皆宇宙であり、ここまで進化してきた存在であり、いつまでも共に存在し続けられるという強い確信をもって、完全にひとつに溶け合っているのだ。— RCR

The cloud woman and cloud woman embody
and represent a vision of the naturalization of humanity.
Man and Woman are a balanced duality
As the recipients of experience, not only in aesthetic-visual terms but
trough the entire body, an awakening of the instincts, a more global,
multi-sensory perception in search of beauty

Cloud Man and Cloud Woman

The Cloud Man and Cloud Woman perform and represent a vision of their renaturalization, a step further in the evolution and awareness of a new reality of realities.

They appear as representatives of the new global era in which the different realities must coexist: the tangible reality, the intangible, and furthermore the virtual one created by man.

They are carriers of a new cosmology and concept of reality in which life has meaning and significance again.

They appear materially diffused, perceived as spectra, as a valley of particles, as an energetic aura, but rather as a mass of constant matter.

They represent the continuous movement, cyclic, the constant change. Life as a rhythm, as a phenomenon that vibrates constantly.

Man and woman as a balanced duality. With a richer and more creative experience from the simplest to the most complex aspects.

We see them as percipients of the experience, not only in an aesthetic and visual sense, but through the whole body, an awakening of all instincts, a more global perception, but multisensory, in search of beauty.

They are representatives of the unit body-mind-consciousness, individual-society and society-nature that gives a new individual and collective consciousness, generating radically new approaches.

In short, they are anthropomorphic models of reference and representatives of the new integral consciousness.

雲男と雲女

雲男と雲女は、人間の自然化に対するビジョンを体現し、象徴するものである。それは進化のもう一歩先にある存在であり、新しい現実に対する意識の表明でもある。

彼らは新しいグローバルな時代を代表する者たちとして現れる。その時代にはふたつの現実が共存している。ひとつは有形の現実、そしてもうひとつは人間がつくり出した仮想現実的な無形の現実である。

彼らは新しい宇宙論と現実的な概念を運ぶ者たちである。そこで人生は再び意味と意義をもつだろう。

それは物質的には拡散しており、一定の質量をもった物質というよりも、スペクトルや粒子の谷、あるいは光るエネルギーのような様相を呈している。

彼らは連続的な動き、周期的な変化、絶え間ない変化の表徴である。リズムとしての、または常に振動する現象としての生命。

男と女とは、バランスの取れた二元性のことである。最も単純なものから最も複雑なものに至るまで、それは豊かさと創造的な体験を伴うものである。

私たちは雲男と雲女を経験の知覚者としてとらえている。美学的、視覚的な意味だけではなく、身体のすべてを通して知覚する者。美を求めて、すべての本能を、全体的な知覚を、より複合的な感覚を目覚めさせる者として。

彼らは、身体と精神と意識を、個人と社会を、あるいは社会を自然を一体化させた存在として、新しい個人と集団の意識を与えてくれる者であり、根本的に新しいアプローチを生み出す者なのである。

要するに、彼らは参照(レファレンス)を擬人化したモデルであり、新たな総合的意識を代表する者たちなのである。

GLOBAL ENDS: Towards the beginning exhibition at TOTO Gallery・MA, 2012

「グローバル・エンズ：始まりに向けて」展会場 TOTOギャラリー・間 2012年

"We have always thought that architecture should be understood within a way of life and as a philosophy of living. We have not separated work from other aspects of ourlives because we have never felt that we were working." RCR

私たちはいつも、建築というものが生き方として、生きるための哲学として理解されるべきだと考えていた。私たちは、仕事とその他の物事を分け隔てたことがない。なぜなら、働いている、と感じたことが一度もないのだから。— RCR

Humanitacle

HUMANITACLE is a word coined by us which wants to express a synthesis project of man and living in relation to landscape and nature.

HUMANITACLE is also a life project as a creative and shared experience in a global way between us and many more in this dream geography.

A new way of understanding the world, man, inhabiting, relationships between people, nature... as a reality to express our cosmology.

It is the place of research, of Laboratory (Lab·A). It is the place of confluence of what we dream, what we investigate and what we build.

An experiential place.

An integral place (to live, to eat, to dress and to generate health). A place of beauty.

A place of expression where architecture and landscape encompass the lives of people.

(Final purpose of the BUNKA foundation: to give value to the architecture.)

Message with universal vocation and open to everyone.

ヒューマニタクル

ヒューマニタクルとは、人間とその住環境を、ランドスケープと自然との関係のなかにおいて統合する、という概念を説明するため、私たちが創った造語である。

と同時にヒューマニタクルとは、総合的な意味において、私たちと、この夢のジオグラフィーのなかにあるさまざまなものの間に起こる、創造的な、そして共有的な経験としての、人生をかけたプロジェクトでもある。

それは世界を、人間を、居住環境を、人と人の間の関係を、そして自然を理解するための新しい方法、私たちの宇宙学を表現するための現実である。

それは探求する場所、研究所（Lab·A）である。そこで、私たちが夢見ること、調べていること、そして建設しているものが合流する。

それは体験的な場所である。

それは一体的な場所（衣食住、そして健康であろうとすること）であり、美しさの場所である。

建築と風景が人びとの生活を取り巻くような、表現の場所である。

（BUNKA財団の最終目的は、建築に価値を与えること）

普遍的な使命をもった、すべての人びとに開かれたメッセージ。

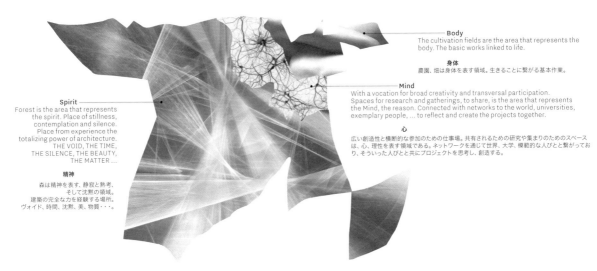

Three areas
Differentiated to make reference to the Body-senses, the Mind-reason and the Spirit

3つの領域
身体-感覚、心-理性、精神に当てられた異なる領域

"We imagine.
The imagination is the start of creation.
We imagine ideas, concepts, not forms,
in the terrain of every possible one.
We make the imagined visible.
We want to turn the imaginary into lines,
into representation. The idea becomes form.
We turn the representation of the imagined
into manifest matter, accompanied.
That becomes the architectural work." RCR

私たちは想像する。
想像することは創造のはじまりである。
私たちは想像する。アイディアを、概念を、かたちではなく、
あらゆるものが可能な領域のなかに。
私たちは想像したものを視覚化する。
私たちは想像したものをいくつかの線に、表現に、変えた
いと願う。そしてアイデアはかたちになる。
私たちは、その、想像されたものの表現を、物質性を伴った
マニフェストに変容させる。それが建築作品なのだ。
── RCR

Concepts of this Territory

このテリトリーの概念

VIVID

It is a living project from the first day, because there is a natural geography and cultural identity.

It is alive because we are already part of it; it is a life project in constant progress and becomes the dream of the next years.

It is alive because people work there (Research Centre), while they are connected in a planetary way.

It is alive because there are always happening things: it is a project with no deadline, in a permanent process of change. (A closed or executed project is dead.)

CREATIVE

It is the place of origin of the cloud man and woman, as creative creatures par excellence and creators of reality.

DIVERS

Wealth is in diversity. Equality does not reside in uniformity, but in the recognition of the value and dignity of the differences of all people and all peoples and cultures. (Social)

SUSTAINABLE, SELF-SUFFICIENT

Only with a sustainable vision can be ensured the survival of man's life.

This site must also be sustainable and self-sufficient to ensure its subsistence and to be simultaneously able to nurture research. (Laboratory)

INTEGRAL

A pioneering site as an example of the unprecedented transformation that is being developed as an integral, unified, holistic, inclusive, interrelated and interconnected whole.

It is a place and experiential laboratory of this integral vision.

生きる

それは一番最初の日から、生きているプロジェクトである。そこには自然の地理的な条件があり、文化的なアイデンティティーが備わっている。

生きている、というのも、私たちはすでにその一部分なのだ。それは常に進歩し続け、これから何年もかけて夢を叶えていく、人生をかけたプロジェクトだ。

生きている、というのは、そこで働くからであり（研究センター）同時に地球全体と繋がっているからなのだ。

生きている、というのは、そこでいつも何かが起こっているからである。完成予定日はなく、プロセスは常に変化し続けるだろう。（閉じた、または遂行されたプロジェクトは死んでいる。）

創造力

そこは現実を創り出す、卓越性を備えた創造的な存在、雲男と雲女の起源となる場所である。

多様性

豊かさは多様性のなかに見出すことができる。平等とは、均一性のなかに宿るものではなく、すべての人びとと、すべての町や村、そしてすべての文化の差異がもつ価値と尊厳を認識するということである。（社会）

持続可能性、自給自足性

持続可能なビジョンだけが人間の生命の存続を保証する。

ここは、その生存を保証し、同時にここでの探求を続けていくことができるよう（研究所）、持続可能性をもち、自給自足できる力を備えた場所となるだろう。

統合

ここは統合的で、包括的、全体的で、受容性、相互関連性と相互接続性の高い、前例のない先駆的な変化し続ける場所である。

ここは、総合的な視野をもった、実験的な研究所なのだ。

"Making a dream come true: discovering a place to dream in, with meetings, debates, conversations, meditation, silence, the garden, history, and... smelling and breathing. Creating: architecture and landscape. Sharing: for us and many others. A place where one can feel the forces of nature, the air, water, earth, vegetation, fire... that imbue our everyday lives and remind us that we are ephemeral and vulnerable, and that make us value what is essential. A place to perform acts of magic, which ultimately is to bring imagination to reality."
RCR

夢を実現すること。それは夢を見るための場所を見つけること。それは人との出会いであり、議論や会話であり、瞑想や沈黙、庭、歴史、そして匂いをかぎ、呼吸することである。
創造すること。建築とランドスケープを。
共有すること。私たちと、他の多くの人たちのために。
夢を見ることができる場所、それは自然や空気、水、土、植物、火などの力を感じることができる場所である。それらは私たちの日常生活のなかにあり、私たちが儚く脆弱な存在であることを思い出させたり、大切なものを見極めさせてくれるものである。それは、魔法を起こすための場所。究極的には、想像したものを現実に変えることなのだ。—— RCR

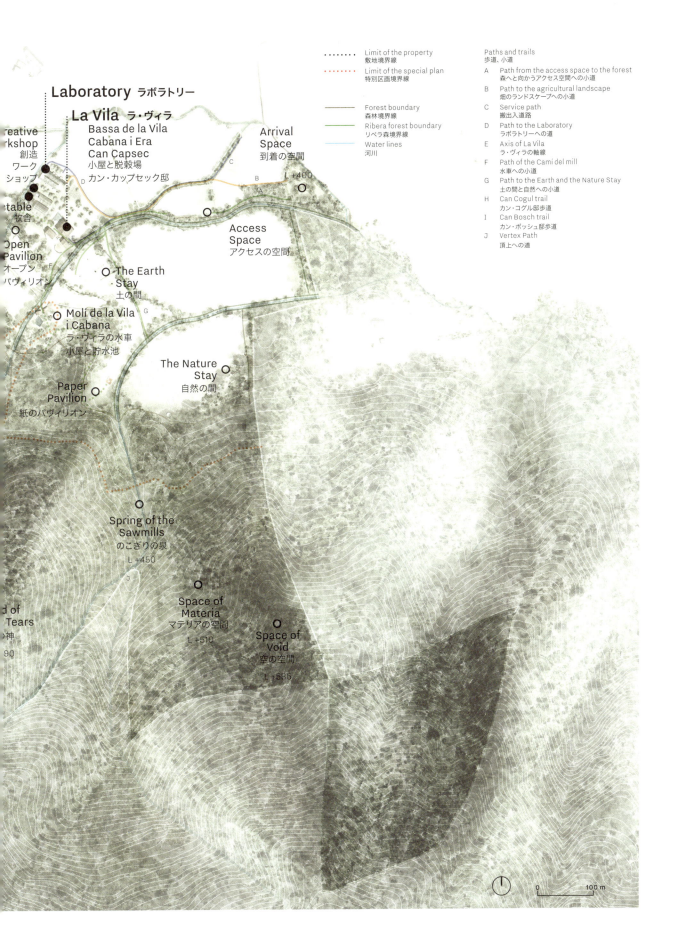

"Our imagination is as real as the world around us; a world of infinite possibilities, because the world is a result of our own imagination and creation. What we believe and feel is reality, it creates and forms our lives. That instant, our life, is nothing more than a blank wall, on which we can imprint our imagination and make our life what we wish it to be." RCR

私たちの想像力は、まわりにあるこの世界と同じくらい現実的なものだ。世界は無限の可能性に満ちている。なぜなら、この世界は私たち自身の想像力と創造の結果なのだから。私たちが信じるもの、感じることは現実であり、それらが私たちの人生をつくる。その瞬間、私たちの人生とはただの白い壁のようなものだということが分かる。そこに私たちの想像を刻み、望むような人生をそこに投影することができるような白い壁だということに。—— RCR

The mechanical laboratory offers spaces for reflection and experimentation for people destined to create.

The chemistry laboratory offers spaces of relationship and understanding for people who are meant to dream.

機械的なラボラトリー。創造する人のために、内省のための空間や実験のための空間をつくることが試みられる。

化学的なラボラトリー。夢を見る人のために、関係性のための空間や、理解のための空間をつくることが試みられる。

Arrival Space

Initial stop where we made the first release, we leave the car in a forest. We feel for the first time that we are in a place of great natural wealth. Everything is quiet, two paths, one that leads to the access space and another that does not.

到着の空間

ここは最初にこの森の世界へと引き込まれた場所、乗って来た車を止めた森である。ここで私たちは初めて自然の壮大な豊かさに触れた。すべてが静寂に包まれたこの場所からは、ふたつの道が続いている、ひとつはアクセスの空間へ続き、もうひとつはそこでない別の場所へと繋がっている。

"Architecture is the art of materialising
  the dreams on a long-distance journey." RCR

建築とは、長きにわたって見る夢を具現化するための技術
である。—— RCR

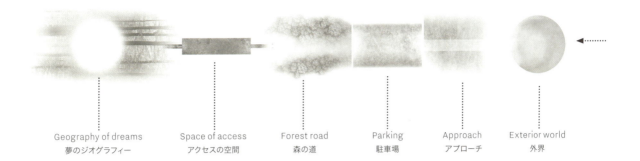

| Geography of dreams | Space of access | Forest road | Parking | Approach | Exterior world |
| 夢のジオグラフィー | アクセスの空間 | 森の道 | 駐車場 | アプローチ | 外界 |

Access Space

The access space is a path where things happen to you. Where you dispose to immerse yourself.

アクセスの空間

アクセスの空間では、何かが訪問者に起こる。その先に入っていくために、自分自身を一旦置いていく場所である。

"Seeking beauty in our daily actions or implementing any activity or project which becomes one of the greatest sources of satisfaction." RCR

私たちが行っている日々の行為、行動、プロジェクトをつくることのなかに美しさを求めることは、満足を得るための最も大きな方法のひとつとなった。— RCR

Research center

WHAT?

Man, as a centre of research linked to the process of evolution of his basic needs, to inhabit, eat and clothing to achieve harmony between the tangible and the intangible.

HOW?

Research area and gatherings, to share. It is the area that represents the mind, the reason, with a vocation of broad creativity and with cross-sectional participation. Connected networked in the world, universities, exemplary people... reflecting and creating projects together.

リサーチ・センター

概要

人間はその存在自体が、衣食住といった基本的要求を満たし、形のあるものとないものの間に調和をもたらすための進化のプロセスと深く関わった研究センターのようなものである。

機能

ここは共有を目的とした研究、集会施設である。それは、心と理を表す領域として、広い意味での創造力に基づき、多岐に渡る専門領域を横断しながら使用される。ここは世界的なネットワーク、大学、志ある人びとが連携しながら、共にプロジェクトを考え、創造していく場所なのである。

"Shared creativity is the kind whose results are greater than the sum of its parts.
It attains results that are more balanced, more reliable than individual reason with no less creative intensity.
To share is to be receptive, to converse, to feel lighter.
To share is to feel mutual enrichment; to feel the presence of the group without being present in it. Is more of a feeling of belonging rather than of authorship.
To share is effort and dedication to ensure that the relationship stays alive and intense." RCR

共有された創造性というのは、部分の合計よりもその総体の方が大きくなるような性質をもつものだ。たとえ個々の創造性の強度が十分に高いものであったとしても、ここでの総体はそういった個人の理よりも、バランスの取れた、より信頼の置けるものになるだろう。
共有するということは、受容的になることであり、対話をすることであり、軽く感じることである。
共有するということは相互に豊かになることを感じることだ。グループのなかに居るのではなく、グループそのものの全体の存在を感じること。誰のものかという著者性を問うのではなく、そこに属していると感じることだ。
共有するということは、そのような関係を生き生きと強いものとして保ち続けるための努力と献身である。 — RCR

Laboratory　　　　　　　　　　　　　　　　　　　　　　　ラボラトリー

Creative box. Autonomous working-meeting cells, for temporary use, that allow the collaboration of external companies for the development of specific projects.

クリエイティブボックス：作業や打ち合わせ用の、自立したセル状の空間ユニット。外部企業との共同作業や、特定のプロジェクトの開発などのためのテンポラリーな使用を想定している。

Creative Workshop　創造ワークショップ

Garden of the Muses　女神たちの庭園

"Architecture is offering someone an
experience of beauty and emotion." RCR

建築は、誰かに美しさと感動という経験を与えている。
— RCR

"We now know that the physical basis of reality is more like clouds or fog than iron or stone. The consequence of this insubstantiality of matter brings us closer to the intangible, and it can enrich our tangible perception of realty with a broad range of nuances." RCR

私たちは現在の現実の物理的な根拠が、鉄や石のようなものではなく雲や霧のようなものだということを知っている。そしてそのように物質が非現実的になると、私たちは無形に近づき、それは私たちの有形に対する感覚をも広いニュアンスをもった豊かなものにしてくれるのだ。— RCR

The Air Stay - Fireflies

The Air Stay are multipurpose cells.

A kind of membrane between Man and Nature.

A protective place to be, sleep, read, think, dream and, at the same time, playful to play ...

These small translucent spaces are invaded by the environment that surrounds them during the day and, at night, they can illuminate the surroundings, like fireflies.

空気の間──蛍

この、多目的に使用するための細胞状の空間は、人間と自然の間の膜のような存在である。

外界から保護されたこの場所で、人は休み、眠り、本を読み、考えをめぐらせ、夢を見、また同時に遊ぶ。

これらの小さな半透明の空間は、昼にはそれを取り囲む環境を内部に浸透させ、そして夜には、蛍のようにその光で周囲を照らし出す。

The Earth Stay

Man lives on earth and raises limits to envelop and create spaces. We want to explore in the Vila the possibility of digging the limits instead of raising them and feeling how to live inside the earth. But going beyond the cave and let natural light bathe spaces and qualify them generating perceptions of depth, calm, elevation, crushing, continuity… a joint modelling between earth and light. And that the landscape is shown as a modelling dotted with imprints.

土の間

人は大地の上に生き、閉じた空間をつくる境界線を立ち上げる。私たちはこのラ・ヴィラで、その境界線を立ち上げるのではなく掘り込むことによって、大地の中に生きる感覚、その可能性を探求したい。それは洞窟を超えた何か、空間に落ちる自然光が、深みや静寂、隆起、破砕、連続を知覚させ、大地と光の間にモデルをつくる。その風景は、大地に点在する刻印のように現れることだろう。

"While we develop our projects, we contemplate the idea presented to us, and if the result is anything but beautiful, we know we must continue." RCR

プロジェクトを展開させながら、私たちはそこに出されたアイディアについて考える。そしてその結果、それが美しいものであれば、それを進めて良いと判断する。— RCR

"Architecture only encloses voids and, as architects, we're interested in defining these voids by establishing a rhythm of matter, a concentration of matter, in the different scales of the intervention." RCR

つまるところ建築とは、空っぽの隙間を包み込むだけのものなのだ。そして私たちは建築家として、そのような空っぽの隙間に物質のリズムを与えたい。その介入におけるさまざまなスケールにおいて物質を凝縮させたいのだ。── RCR

The Wood Stay

The forest also looks, like in the framing of a panoramic camera, at two hills. The stay simply looks.

Its wooden structure, its railing and its line of water make up a space discovered, covered and closed, between the forest and the horizon, where to live and share work and dream.

Sober in its approach and in its means, it is linked to the spirit of those who live in it and feel close to the spirit of nature.

木の間

森も、ものを見る。それはパノラマ写真を撮影するカメラのように、ふたつの丘の上で風景を切り取っている。それはそこにあり、ただ、ものを見ている。

その木構造、手すり、そして水の流れは、森と地平線の間に見出され、屋根を架けられ、閉じられたひとつの空間をつくる。それは共有され、仕事をし、夢を見るために使用される。

それは、そのアプローチとその手段において、自然を身近に感じるその空間の住民の精神と結びついている。

Paper Pavilion   紙のパビリオン

The project of the PAPER PAVILION is presented in the framework of the Geography of Dreams.

As a tribute to the forests of YOSHINO, the Buddhist monk and poet Thich Nhat Hanh, and the carpenter Tsunebazu Nishioka.

To the tree that can generate such a special material, wood, which can build large temples, homes and at the same time something as fragile as paper; so that, among others, poets can develop poetry.

(It is an implicit tribute to the entire Japanese wood culture.)

It is a wooden pavilion, with an exterior base. In the central part of the pavilion there would be a small cedar, and it would be taken care so that it grows, when being a little bigger it would be replanted, the action would be repeated and this would create a cedar forest of the whole world with a centenary and Millenarian vocation, as a message of hope, and as a sign of the necessary effort to protect this fundamental legacy that is nature.

(Indirectly we show the value of the management of the Yoshino forests with more than 500 years, as an example and a hopeful sustainable response for a world that is still possible.)

In addition, he will house the complete "no paper" poem by Thich Nhat Hanh and the PRITZKER speech, as well as Yoshino walls and forests in relation to photography of the location landscape of the paper pavilion.

夢のジオグラフィーの枠組みのなかに、この紙のパビリオンのプロジェクトは提示される。

これは吉野の森、仏教の僧侶でもあり詩人でもあるティク・ナット・ハン、そして大工の西岡常一氏へのひとつのオマージュである。

木には、木材という特別な素材を生み出す能力が備わっている。木材を使うことで、大きな寺社や住宅をつくることも、紙のような薄くはかないものをつくることもできる。

(同時にこれは、日本における木の文化すべてに対する暗黙のオマージュでもある。)

それは実際には木製のパビリオンである。その内部の中央には小さな杉の苗木が植えられ、大事に育てられる。ある程度成長したら、その苗木は森へと移植される。そしてまた小さな苗木を育てる。これを繰り返して100年後、1000年後に杉の森を世界に育てたい。それは希望に満ちたメッセージである。自然、というもっとも基本的で重要な私たちの遺産を、世話し守り続けていくために必要な努力を示すという意味で。

(このことは間接的に、500年以上にわたって吉野の人たちが彼らの森を管理し続けてきたことがもつ価値を指し示している。それは持続可能な世界をつくることが今でもまだ可能であるということを示す事例であり、希望でもある。)

その内部空間には、吉野杉でつくられる壁の上に、ティク・ナット・ハンの詩「紙でないもの」の全文と、プリツカー賞受賞時のスピーチが掲示され、紙のパビリオンが建つ土地の風景写真と共に吉野の森との関係が明らかになるだろう。

"The logic of the living is always systemic. The most emblematic examples are architectures that are blurred on the borderline between architecture and urbanism, architecture and landscape, architecture and nature, in short, between architecture and humanity." RCR

生きるものの論理というのは常に全体的なものだ。そのもっとも象徴的な例は、建築と都市の間の境界、建築とランドスケープの間の境界、建築と自然の間の境界があいまいな建築である。つまりそこでは建築と人間性との間に境界がほとんどないのである。— RCR

La Vila

Yoshino

"The few words that define the works are
 metaphors. Architecture is not understood
 as a treaty of geometry and construction,
 but rather as the materialisation of a feeling,
 of a vital instant, of an idea, of that feeling that
 it takes form and value from life." RCR

少ない言葉で作品を定義しようとすると、それはメタファと
なる。建築は形態や建設手法の合意点として理解されるも
のではなく、むしろ決定的な瞬間に沸き起こる感情やひと
つのアイディア、または人生のなかに見出せる価値などを物
質化したものなのである。— RCR

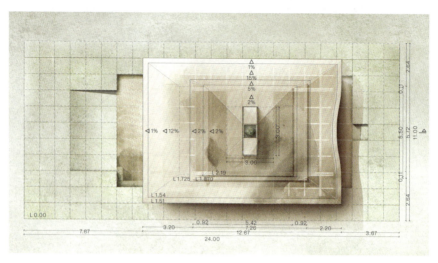

Roof plan

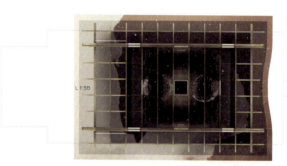

Ceiling plan

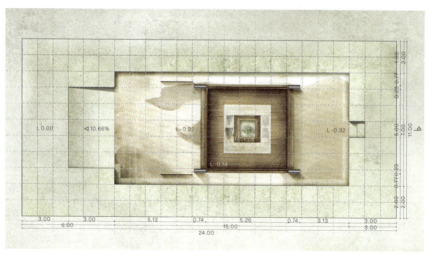

Ground floor plan

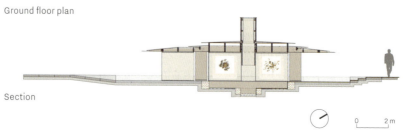

Section

Professor Kazuki Maeda came to Olot to show us his work with paper. What he presented us not only did not leave us indifferent, but we saw a source of great creative wealth because he explored the work of making paper in large format and also explored how paper from his own process emerged already painted. That the very mass of the paper contained the painting, the drawing or the transparency was really unique.

After further discussions we decided to organize together for the next summer, coinciding with the workshop we organize every year, a few days in the Vila to create in situ and in a communal way, the large sheets of paper in one piece, which will configure the enclosures of the homonymous pavilion that is going to be built in the Vila thanks to the collaboration of Yoshino's carpenters, reinforcing even more, if possible, the relations between RCR and Japan.

前田一樹教授がオロットに来て、彼の作品である紙を私たちに見せてくれた。それは私たちの関心を大いに惹きつけただけでなく、巨大な紙をつくり、自ら開発した手法で着彩された紙を漉くという探求力によって、素晴らしい創造性の豊かさを見ることになった。紙の繊維そのものの中に模様が含まれているその様子、絵柄や透明感は本当に今まで見たことのないものであった。

その後話し合いを重ね、私たちは来年の夏に一緒に紙をつくることを決めた。私たちが毎年行っているワークショップに合わせて、ラ・ヴィラで、2、3日かけて皆で大きな1枚の紙をつくるのだ。その紙は、吉野の大工たちの協力によって、ラ・ヴィラに建設される予定の紙のパビリオンを包むような何かになるだろう。そのことによって、RCRと日本との関係が、より一層強いものとなってくれることを願っている。

"A good project needs reasons, explanations and comments. A profound project touches the senses and thoughts start firing off. A beautiful project, when it emerges, can only be felt; it brings joy and there are no regrets."
RCR

良いプロジェクトは、理由、説明、コメントを必要とする。深いプロジェクトは感覚に触れ、思考を刺激する。だが美しいプロジェクトは、それが現れるとき、ただ感じることだけしかできないものである。それは喜びをもたらし、悔いを残さない。── RCR

The Cosmology of RCR

Architectural creations, like all human endeavours, are born from an inner ocean made of currents of longings, feelings and all manner of experiences: our works and actions are like flecks of foam splashing as the waves of that ocean break against the cliffs and beaches of material reality. The waves are superficially shaped by the world's winds, but they are also influenced by the invisible currents of our values and beliefs, and, at a deeper level, by a worldview, or cosmology, which is generally implicit and unconscious. Sometimes it is useful to make this cosmology or worldview more explicit. This will be the aim that RCR do inside of the Paper Pavilion space.

RCR sees the nascent project at La Vila as "a dream of architecture and life": a creative centre for research, experience and vital learning, "with a humanistic and transdiciplinary vocation", and open to people from around the world. The main star guiding this project is the need, given the challenges and convulsions of our time, to develop a new awareness in relation to our dwelling, to our sense of place and to our own experience.

Jordi Pigem Philosopher

RCRのコスモロジー

建築作品は、他のすべての人間活動と同じように、憧れ、感情、そしてあらゆる種類の経験が渦巻く内なる大海のなかで生まれる。私たちのつくる作品と行動とは、この海の波が物質的な現実の岩石に当たって弾けたときに現れる泡のようなものだ。これらの波は、世界の風の影響を受けてその水面の形を変え、同時に私たちの価値観や信念といった目に見えない流れの影響を受け、そしてそのもっと底深いところでは、一般に無意識で暗黙のものと考えられているような、世界観によって動かされている。しばしば、こういった世界や宇宙の明示的な見方をすることが有用である。それこそが、RCRがこの紙のパヴィリオンの空間内において行おうとしていることだ。

RCRは、「建築と人生の夢」として、このラ・ヴィラのプロジェクトを構想している。それは「人間的な、そして横断的な職業的意識をもって」真に重要なことを研究し、体験し、学ぶための、世界に対して開かれたセンターである。このプロジェクトにおいて私たちを導く星の役割を担うものは、現代世界で私たちが抱えている課題と動乱を意識しながら、場所に対する感覚に向かって、自分自身で経験しながら住むことに向かって新たな知覚を開くための、必要性である。

哲学者　ジョルディ・ピジェム

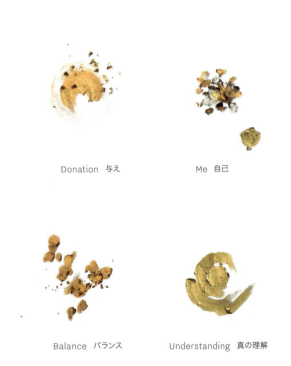

Flow　流れ   Project　投影   Donation　与え   Me　自己

Polarity　極性   Complexity　複雑性   Balance　バランス   Understanding　真の理解

Concepts that I see as essential in the cosmology: life-attitude of RCR

このコスモロジーにおいて最も本質的なもの：RCRの人生に対する姿勢

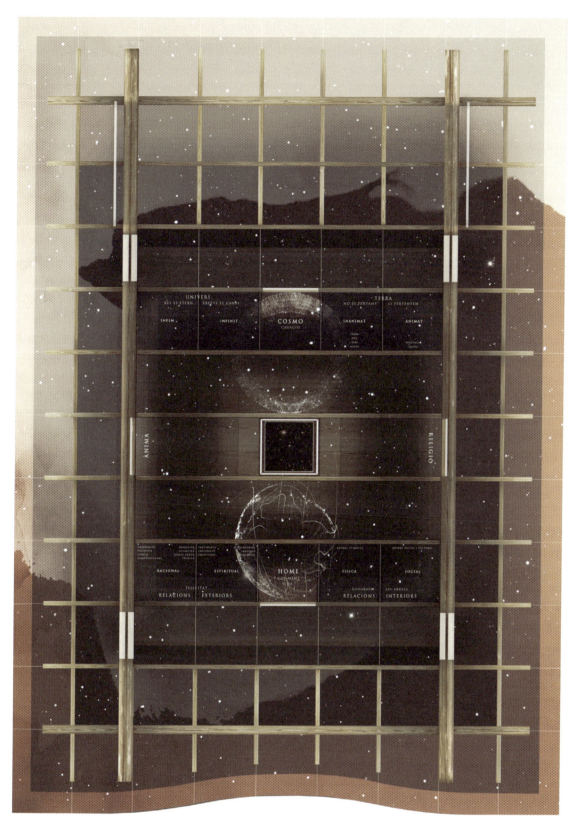

Ceiling of the *Pavilion of Paper*

Sin título, Series Japón, 2017
Gouache with ink on Caballo 109A paper 250g/m²
Polyptych composed of papers measuring
70x100cm: 280x100cm. Series 1, May 27th, 2017

無題、シリーズ「日本」2017年
不透明水彩絵の具、Caballo 109A 250g/m² 紙使用
複数枚による構成 70x100cm：280x100cm
シリーズ1、2017年5月27日

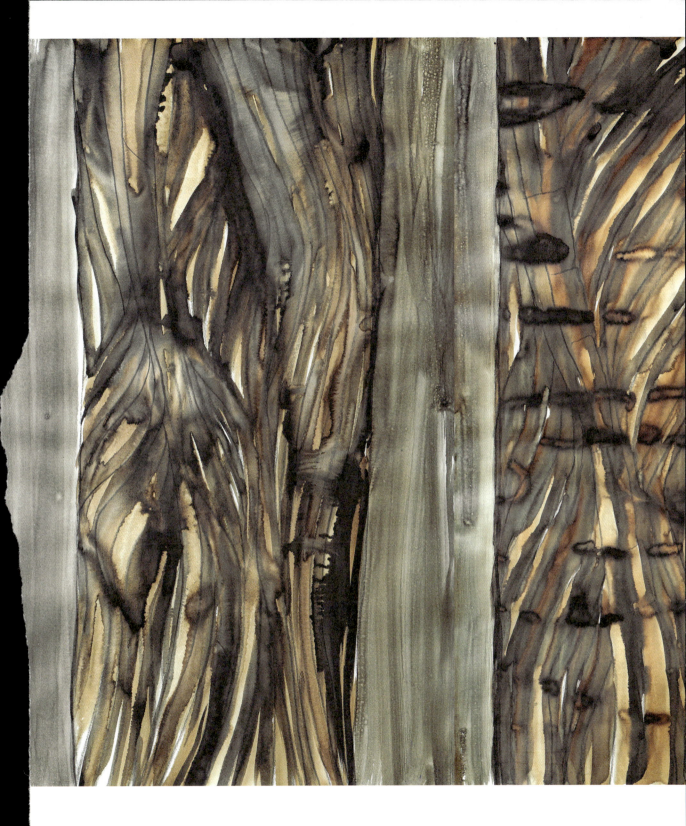

"It is the architecture that places meaning
in specific places and the experience lived by
its implantation and espaciality to stimulate
the imagination and call to dream" RCR

ある特定の場所に意味を与えるもの、それを置くことによっ
て経験が生きたものとなること、その空間によって想像力
が刺激され、夢を大きな声で語りたくなるもの、それこそが
建築なのだ。── RCR

"The outline that for years has allowed us to present the strength of a concept in a synthesized, suggesting way. A concept that may be on different scales, or in different stages of the project. A brush, sometimes thick, others thin, dipped in ink, one moment black, the next full of colour, usually on a sketch drawn in pencil by a determined hand which allows the vibrant technique and the dynamic shapes and strokes to express infinite suggestions: ultimately, illustrating the project in creative calligraphy." RCR

長年にわたって、コンセプトの強さを総合的に、示唆的に提示するために線画を利用してきた。それらのコンセプトはスケールも違えば、プロジェクトにおける段階も異なっている。その筆使いは、時には太く、時には細く、インクを用いたり、黒を使うこともあればさまざまな色を用いられることもある。普段は鉛筆を使って一気に描く。固有の技術、ダイナミックな形、ストロークを使うことで無限の提案を表現できるように。究極的には、プロジェクトを描くという行為は、創造的な書、カリグラフィーなのである。— RCR

"The ability to distinguish wood and trees
with clarity is a capacity for silence, to silence
everything that is not essential" RCR

木と森を見分ける能力、というのは明らかに沈黙の能力の
ことである。それは本質的なもの以外のすべてのものを沈
黙させるということだ。— RCR

Yoshino

"We are dreamers and we specialize in
making them come true, that is our heritage.
Architecture is the art of making all that
we imagine visible, physical." RCR

夢想家としてその夢を実現させることを仕事にしている、と
いうのが私たちの立ち位置である。建築とは、私たちが想
像するすべてを物理的に、目に見えるものとしてつくり上げ
るための技術である。── RCR

La Vila

"It is the architecture that places meaning
in specific places and the experience lived by
its implantation and espaciality to stimulate
the imagination and call to dream" RCR

ある特定の場所に意味を与えるもの、それを置くことによっ
て経験が生きたものとなること、その空間によって想像力
が刺激され、夢を大きな声で語りたくなるもの、それこそが
建築なのだ。— RCR

"It may be a good thing, at times, to forget everything we have been taught, to close our eyes and imagine new architecture, which in reality is all around us, in our everyday perception of every natural phenomenon, flowers, trees, mountains, clouds..." RCR

時には、私たちがこれまでに教えられてきたすべてのことを一度忘れてみるとよい。目を閉じて、新しい建築を想像してみる。それは実際にはどこにでもあるものであり、花や木々、山々や雲などの自然を前にしたときに感じるような、私たちの日常の知覚のなかに、存在しているものなのだ。
— RCR

Projects Maps 作品マップ
La Garrotxa ガロッチャ

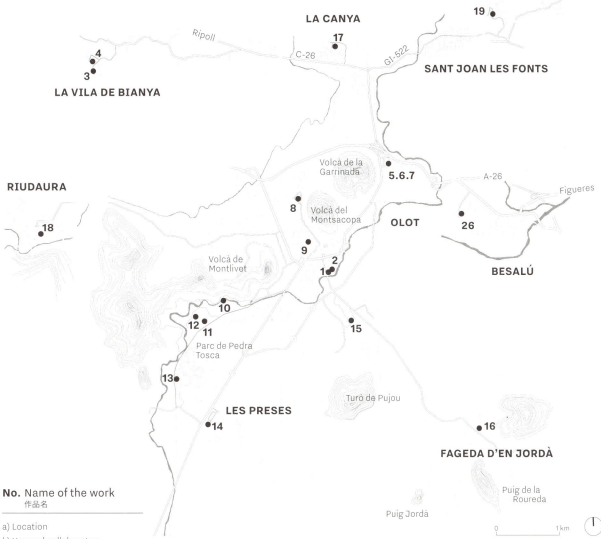

No. Name of the work
作品名

a) Location
b) Use and collaborators
c) Project and construction period
d) Visitors' information

1. Barberí space
バルベリ・スペース

a) C. Fontanella. 26. Olot, Girona
b) Architecture workshop and exhibition space
c) Project 2004-6. Construction 2006-
d) Book visit
visites@rcrbunkafundacio.cat

2. BUNKA Foundation: RCR Arquitectes Founds
BUNKA財団

a) C. Fontanella. 21. Olot, Girona
b) Culture building
c) Project 2013. Construction 2013
d) Book visit
visites@rcrbunkafundacio.cat

3. Vila: the dream of RCR
ラ・ヴィラ

a) La Vila. Vall de Bianya, Girona
c) Project 2002. Construction 2002-3
New Project 2017-
d) Book visit
www.rcrlaba.cat

4. Pond in La Vila de Trincheria
トリンチェリア、ラ・ヴィラの池

a) GIP-5222. 17813 La Vila de Vianya
(42.2097N 2.42208E)
c) Project 2013. Construction 2013
d) Book visit and accommodation
www.rcrlaba.cat
visites@rcrbunkafundacio.cat

"In love there is no need for words: silent
  comprehension goes beyond language" RCR

愛は、言葉を必要としない。沈黙のうちに生じる深い理解
は、言葉を超える。— RCR

5. Les Cols Restaurant
ラス・コルス・レストラン

a) Crta. de La Canya, s/n. Olot, Girona
b) Restaurant renovation and addition
c) Project 2001-2. Construction 2002-3
d) Interior visit only for customers

6. Les Cols Pavilions
ラス・コルス・パヴィリオン

a) Crta. de La Canya, s/n. Olot, Girona
b) Hotel rooms
c) Project 2002-3. Construction 2004-5
d) Interior visit only for customers

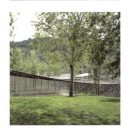

7. Marquee for Les Cols Restaurante
ラス・コルス・レストランの大テント

a) Crta. de La Canya, s/n. Olot, Girona
b) Celebration space
c) Project 2007-9. Construction 2009-11
d) Interior visit only for customers

8. Margarida House
マルガリーダ・ハウス

a) C. Sant Julià de Mont, 12. Olot, Girona
b) Single-family dwelling
c) Project 1988-9. Construction 1989-92
d) Exterior visit only

9. Space Volcano
スペース・ボルケーノ

a) El Firal i Firalet. Olot, Girona
b) Public space
c) 1st Prize Competition 2003. Project 2004-8. Construction 2009-10 1st Phase
d) Open access

10. Bathing Pavilion
水浴パヴィリオン

a) Tossols-Basil. Parc Natural de la zona Volcànica de la Garrotxa. Olot, Girona
b) Fluvial services installations
c) Project 1995. Construction 1998
d) Open access

11. Athletics stadium Tossols-Basil
トゥッソル・バジル陸上競技場

a) Tossols-Basil. Parc Natural de la zona Volcànica de la Garrotxa. Olot, Girona
c) Project 1991. Construction 1999-2001
   Project 2009. Construction 2009-12
d) Open access

12. 2x1 Pavilion
2×1パヴィリオン

a) Tussols-Basil. Parc Natural de la zona Volcànica de la Garrotxa. Olot, Girona
b) Football field and bar
c) Project 1999. Construction 2000
d) Open access

13. Pedra Tosca Park
ペドラ・トスカ・パーク

a) Parc de Pedra Tosca. Parc Natural de la zona Volcànica de la Garrotxa. Les Preses, Girona
b) Entry and pathway in a protected area
c) Project 1998-2002. Construction 2003-4
d) Open access

14. Bellows House
ふいごの家

a) Crta. Volcà Racó. Les Preses, Girona
b) Single-family dwelling
c) Project 1997-8. Construction 1998-2001
d) Exterior visit only

15. Panoramic House
ミラドール・ハウス（見晴台の家）

a) Crta. Comercial GI-524. Olot, Girona
b) Single-family dwelling
c) Project 1994. Construction 1997-9
d) Exterior visit only

16. Entry pavilion to the Fageda d'en Jordà
ファジェダ・ダン・ジョルダのエントランス・パヴィリオン

a) Crta. GE-524. Olot-Sta. Pau Km4 Parc Natural de la zona Volcànica de la Garrotxa. Olot, Girona
c) Project 1993. Construction 1994
d) Open access

17. House for an Ironmanger and a Hairdresser
鍛冶屋と美容師の家

a) Urb. La Roureda, Illa D. La Canya, Girona
b) Single-family dwelling
c) Project 1996-98. Construction 1999-2000
d) Exterior visit only

18. M-Lidia House
M-リディア・ハウス

a) Urb. la Cometa, C. Sant Grau, 15. 17855. Montagut, Girona
b) Single-family dwelling
c) Project 2000. Construction 2001-2
d) Exterior visit only

Catalonia　カタルーニャ

--- Route 1: Barcelonès-Osona-Ripollès-Garrotxa
---- Route 2: Barcelonès-Selva-Gironès-Baix i Alt Empordà

23. Els Colors Nursery
アルス・コロールス保育園

a) C. del Ter, 52-54. 08560 Manlleu
b) For children from 0 to 3 years
c) Project 2005-7. Construction 2007-9
d) Visit by appointment
www.manlleu.cat

24. La Lira teatre public space
ラ・リラ・シアター・パブリック・スペース

a) C. Mossèn Cinto Verdaguer, 4. 17500. Ripoll
b) In collaboration: J.Puigcorbè
c) Project 2003-5. Construction 2005-11
d) Open access

25. Recreation and Culture Zones
レクリエーション、文化施設

a) Plaça del Gambeto 1. Riudaura, Girona
b) Civic center
c) Project 1994-6. Construction 1997-9
d) Exterior visit only

19. Office Building Plaça Europa 31
オフィス・ビル・プラサ・エウロパ31

a) Av. Joan Carles I. 08908 L'Hospitalet de Llobregat, Barcelona
b) Building for rent offices
c) Project 2002-4. Construction 2005-7
d) Exterior visit only

26. El Petit Comte Nursery
ペティット・コムテ保育園

a) C. Jacint Verdaguer. 17850 Besalú, Girona
c) Project 2005-7. Construction 2007-9
d) Visit by appointment
www.besalu.cat

20. Sant Antoni-Joan Oliver library
サン・アントーニ――ジョアン・オリヴェール図書館

a) C. Comte Borrell, 44-46. 08015 Barcelona
b) Recovery of public spaces
c) Project 2002-4. Construction 2005-7
d) Visit according to schedule

27. Law Faculty, University of Girona
ジローナ大学法学部棟

a) C. Universitat de Girona, 12. 17071 Girona
c) Project 1995-6. Construction 1997-9
d) Visit by appointment
www.udg.edu

21. Enigma Restaurant
エニグマ・レストラン

a) C. Sepúlveda, 38-40. 08015 Barcelona
b) Adrià's Restaurante in collaboration: P. Llimona
c) Project 2014-5. Construction 2015-6
d) Visit only for customers

28. Pavilion on a Pond
池のパヴィリオン

a) C. del Porxo, 1. 17240 Llagostera, Girona
b) Single-family dwelling
c) Project 2001-4. Construction 2004-8
d) Staying service by appointment
www.pabellonenelestanque.com

22. Manlleu Indoor Swimming Pool
マンリェウ屋内スイミング・プール

a) Ctra. de Roda, 1. 08560 Manlleu
c) Project 2001-2. Construction 2004-6
d) Visit by appointment
www.manlleu.cat

29. Lotus Blau Shades Spaces
ロータス・ブラウ・シェード・スペース

a) Veïnat de Vall, s/n. 17430 Santa Coloma de Farners, Girona
b) Celebration space
c) Project 2005. Construction 2007
d) Visit only for customers

30. IES Vilartagues
ヴィラルタガス高校校舎

a) C. Canigó, 41. 17220 Sant Feliu de Guixols
c) Project 1995-7. Construction 1997-9
d) Visit by appointment
www.xtec.cat/iessantfeliu

31. Mas El Vent Meeting Point
マス・エル・ヴェント集会所

a) Ctra. Sant Esteve, 3. 17230 Palamós
b) Rehabilitation of farmhouse
c) Project 2004-5. Construction 2005-10
d) Staying service by appointment
www.brugarol.com/en/mas-del-vent/

32. Bell-lloc Cellars
ベル=リョク・ワイナリー

a) Camí de Bell-Lloc, s/n. 17230 Palamós
b) Private production of wines and cavas
c) Project 2003-5. Construction 2005-7
d) Staying service by appointment
www.fincabell-lloc.com

France, Belgium
フランス、ベルギー

33. Sphere of Light
光の球

a) Port de Palamós. 17230 Palamós
b) Port marker
c) Project 1996-9. Construction 2000
d) Open access

34. La Arboleda Park
ラ・アルボレダ・パーク

a) C. de Carles de Viladomeny. 17255 Begur
c) Project 1998-2001. Construction 2003-5
d) Open access

37. Le Cuisine Art Center
ラ・キュイジーヌ・アート・センター

a) Castell de Nègrepelisse – Place du Château. 82800 Nègrepelisse
b) Center of art and design - associate architect: G.Trégouët (RCR)
c) Project 2009-12. Construction 2012-4
d) Visit according to schedule
www.la-cuisine.fr

38. Gallery, workshop and housing
ギャラリー、ワークショップ、住宅

a) Rue Marengo, 19. 33000 Bordeaux
b) Mixed use - RCR Artotec
c) Project 2012. Construction 2013-6
d) Visit by appointment
tel: +33 0556 467 260

35. Ecole du soleil School complex
エコール・ドゥ・ソレイユ校舎

a) Avenue du 19 Mars 1962. 66120 Font Romeu, France
b) Associate architect: G.Trégouët (RCR)
c) Project 2010-2. Construction 2012-4
d) Visit by appointment
tel: +33 468 300 885

36. Soulages Museum
スーラージュ美術館

a) Jardin du Foirail, avenue Victor Hugo. 12000 Rodez, France
b) Pierre Soulages museum - associate architect: G.Trégouët (RCR)
c) Project 2008-11. Construction 2011-4
d) Visit according to schedule
www.musee-soulages.grand-rodez.com

39. Crematorium Hofheide
オフェイドゥの火葬場

a) Jennekensstraat 5, 3221 Nieuwrode, Belgium
b) In collaboration: Coussée&Goris Architecten
c) Project 2006-08. Construction 2010-4
d) Visit by appointment www.hofheide.be

40. Waalse Krook Mediatheque
ヴァールゼ・クローク・メディアテーク

a) De Waalse Krook. 9000 Gent, Belgium
b) New library and multimedia center in collaboration: Coussée&Goris Architecten
c) Project 2010-3. Construction 2013-7
d) Visit according to schedule
www.opening.dekrook.be

RCR Aranda Pigem Vilalta Arquitectes

A creative architecture studio founded in Olot in 1988 by Rafael Aranda (1961), Carme Pigem (1962), and Ramon Vilalta (1960), has been recognized with many national and international awards. Most recently, the 2017 Pritzker Prize.
In the past, they were recipients of the National Culture Award for Architecture 2005 in Catalonia or Chevalier and Officier de l'Ordre des Arts et des Letters (2008 and 2014), Honorary Fellows by the American Institute of Architecture (AIA, 2010), Honorary Fellows by the Royal Institute of British Architecture (RIBA, 2012) among many others. Since 2008 they have had their headquarters at Espai Barberí, a former an art foundry.
In 2013 they created the RCR BUNKA Foundation to support architecture, landscape, arts and culture throughout society. And in 2017 the laboratory RCR LAB·A located at La Vila, a project in progress, with the collaboration of many, among which the town of Yoshino in Nara, Japan. Major works include the Athletics stadium Tossols-Basil (Olot, Spain. 1991–2012), La Lira theatre public space (Ripoll, Spain. 2011), Soulages Museum (Rodez, France. 2014), and Waalse Krook Mediatheque (Gent, Belgium. 2017).

RCR アランダ・ピジェム・ヴィラルタ・アーキテクツ

1988年にラファエル・アランダ（1961年ー）、カルマ・ピジェム（1962年ー）、ラモン・ヴィラルタ（1960年ー）の3人によりスペイン、オロットに設立された建築創造スタジオ。2017年のプリツカー建築賞をはじめ、2005年カタルーニャ州政府による建築文化賞、フランス芸術文化勲章シュヴァリエ（2008年）およびオフィシエ（2014年）、AIA名誉フェロー（2010年）、RIBA名誉フェロー（2012年）など国内外に多数の受賞歴をもつ。2008年よりその拠点を、旧彫刻鋳造工場であったバルベリ・スペースへと移し、2013年にRCR BUNKA財団（日本語の「文化」に由来）を設立して以来、建築とランドスケープ、アートや文化と社会との関わりの促進に寄与する活動を続けている。
奈良県吉野町をはじめ多くの人びととの協力を得て、RCR LAB・A建築研究所を2017年より進行中のプロジェクトである「ラ・ヴィラ」内に置く。代表作に、「トゥッソル・バジル陸上競技場」（スペイン、オロット、1991－2012年）、「ラ・リラ・シアター・パブリック・スペース」（スペイン、リポイ、2011年）、「スーラージュ美術館」（フランス、ロデーズ、2014年）、「ヴァールゼ・クローク・メディアテーク」（ベルギー、ゲント、2017年）など。

Credit of the works

Athletics stadium Tossols-Basil
Client: Ajuntament d'Olot / Consell Català de l'Esport. Generalitat de Catalunya. Architects: RCR Arquitectes (Rafael Aranda, Carme Pigem, Ramon Vilalta). Collaborators: M.Tàpies, A.Sáez. M.Bordas (Project); Brufau, Obiol, Moya (Structure); G.Rodriguez (Model) Quantity surveyor: P.Rifà. Constructor: Coempco

La Lira theatre public space
Client: Ajuntament de la Comtal Vila de Ripoll. Architects: RCR Arquitectes (Rafael Aranda, Carme Pigem, Ramon Vilalta)/J.Puigcorbé. Collaborators: J.Puigcorbé/ K.Fujii, A.Malaspina (Competition); J.Puigcorbé (Project); Blázquez-Guanter Arquitectes (Structure); PGI (Installations); E.Subirah (Model); K.Norrinder (Visualization). Construction management: J.Puigcorbé / RCR. Quantity surveyor: M.Ortega. Constructor: Asmitec, SL

Bell-lloc Cellars
Client: Explotaciones agrícolas y forestales Brugarol, S.A. Architects: RCR Arquitectes (Rafael Aranda, Carme Pigem, Ramon Vilalta).Collaborators: G.Puigvert, A.Lippmann (Project); Blázquez-Guanter Arquitectes (Structure); BT Enginyeria (Installations); A.Lippmann (Model); A.Lippmann (Visualization). Construction management: RCR, A.Lippmann, G.Puigvert. Quantity surveyor: M.Ortega. Constructor: Floret, SL/ Serralleria Met. F. Collell, SL

Sant Antoni - Joan Oliver library, senior center and Cándida Pérez gardens
Client: Proeixample. Ajuntament de Barcelona. Architects: RCR Arquitectes (Rafael Aranda, Carme Pigem, Ramon Vilalta). Collaborators: O.Gallez, G.Tregouët (Competition); G.Tregouët (Project manager); C.Marzo-Proeixample-, S.Yoshida, A.Beele, M.Gonçalves (Project); Blázquez-Guanter Arquitectes (Structure); Grau-Del Pozo Enginyers SC (Installations); G.Tregouët (Model); M.M.Guaragna, M.Braga (Visualization). Construction management: RCR, G.Tregouët, A.Sáez. Quantity surveyor: GPO: C.Carrasco. Constructor: Vias y Construcciones, SA

Soulages Museum
Client: Grand Rodez. M.Censi, L.Mouly, M.Daures, M.Gosselin, N.Delclaux, B.Decron, Y.Pennec. Architects: RCR Arquitectes (Rafael Aranda, Carme Pigem, Ramon Vilalta)/ G.Trégoüet, Passelac & Roques Architects. Collaborators: D.Delarue, J.Puigcorbé, L.Rotoli, K.Fujii, A.Moura, A.Paulicelli, C.Kuczynski, A.Müller, S.Tarradas, A.Jacunskaite, O.Nouska. Construction management: RCR, G.Tregouët, A.Sáez. Quantity surveyor: GPO: C.Carrasco. Constructor: Vias y Construcciones, SA

Crematorium Hofheide
Client: Intercommunale IGS Hofheide. Architects: RCR Arquitectes (Rafael Aranda, Carme Pigem, Ramon Vilalta)/Coussée & Goris architecten. Collaborators: L.Bjerregaard, M.Cottone, F.De Bruyn, D.Delarue, K.Fujii, A.Heck, G.Ollivier, D.Vens, E.Verstraete, H.Vojtová (Competition);M.Cottone, M.De Waele, K.Van Nieuwenhuyze, C.Wittenbech (Project); CVBA Mouton (Structure); VK Engineering (Installations); G&V bvba (Economy and technical assistance); Raum+Akustik: C.Niederstätter, G.Dissegna (Acoustics); Maquet3 (Model); F.De Bruyn, G.Ollivier, F.Faustino, E.Verstraete (Visualization). Construction management: M.De Waele, K.Van Nieuwenhuyse / G&V: E.Geens

Waalse Krook Mediatheque
Client: CVBA Waalse Krook – Stad Gent. Provincie Oost-Vlaanderen. Universiteit Gent. Instituut voor Breedbandtechnologie. Architects: RCR Arquitectes (Rafael Aranda, Carme Pigem, Ramon Vilalta)/Coussée & Goris architecten. Collaborators: L.Cazala, G. De Cock, F. De Bruyn, J. De Schepper, D.Delarue, J.Feijó, C.Garric, M.Kielian, R.Kobayashi, A.Moura, C.Onisiforou, M.Rodríguez, E.Verschueren,E.Verstraete, Exedra: A.Arraut, A.Buendía, A.Lippmann, P.Rodríguez, C.Torio (Competition); L.Cazala, F.De Bruyn, G.De Cock, J.De Schepper,D.Delarue, J.Feijó, C.Garric, M.Kielian, R.Kobayashi, A.Moura, C.Onisiforou, M.Rodríguez, E.Verstraete, F.Verschueren / Exedra: A.Arraut, A.Buendía,A.Lippmann, P.Rodríguez, C.Torio, G.De Cock, T.Deltour, E.Verstraete (Masterplan); R.Bouciqué, L.De Groote, G.De Vriese, G.Puigvert, S.Tarradas, K.Van Nieuwenhuyze, V.Van Roy / C&V: E.Geens, I.Temmerman / Exedra: A.Arraut, A.Buendía, A.Dalmasas, D.Delarue, A.Lippmann, H.Pires, A.Vicente-Arche (Project); CVBA Mouton (Structure); VK Engineering (Installations); Artec3 Studio (Illumination); G&V bvba (Economy and technical assistance); Raum+Akustik: C.Niederstätter, G.Dissegna /Blasco acoustic design & engineering (Acoustics); Digipoli (ICT); TV Aries-Advisers (Project manager and Quantity surveyor); Evolta (Security coordination); ABO (Geotechnics); SECO (Quality control); S.Tarradas, N.Lopes, F.Faustino / Encaix comunicació visual SL (Model); M.Casas, G.De Cock, J.De Schepper, T.Deltour, O.Gábor, A.Moura, J.Pailleux, E. Verstraete / SBDA (Visualization); S.Tarradas (Furniture and signage). Construction management: L.De Groote, K.Van Nieuwenhuyze / G&V: E.Geens, J.Geens, I. Temmerman

Credit of the book

© of the contents and the project of La Vila
 RCR BUNKA Fundació Privada
© of the texts
 Ken Tadashi Oshima (p. 6-19)
 Josep Maria Montaner
 (p. 24, 38, 56, 76, 102, 138, 172)
 Jordi Pigem (p. 366)
© of the photographic images
 Hisao Suzuki, except
 Robert Prat (p. 34),
 Eduard Mas Deu (p. 244, 261),
 Pep Sau (3 images below on p. 339)

Technical drone assistance:
 Pol Fernandez (p.210-211)
Photo Color Correction:
 Gràfiques Ortells, Barcelona
Translation:
 Catalan / Spanish to English:
 Andrea Buchner (p. 207, 218, 265, 266,
 303, 307, 311, 319, 321, 325, 329, 332, 339,
 341, 351, 353, 363)
 English to Japanese:
 Jun Doi (p. 7-19)
 Catalan / Spanish to Japanese:
 Tomoko Sakamoto (except p. 7-19)

Author of the drawings and sketches:
 RCR Arquitectes
Author of the rendered images:
 RCR Arquitectes (Filipe Nunes, Pablo
 Manteca, Roman Joliy, Alberto Martin,
 Marc Valero, Sophie Mayer)

Data source of the maps (p. 249):
 Institut cartogràfic i geològic de Catalunya
 (ICGC),
 Geòlogic de Catalunya
Illustrations:
 Toni Tort and Ester Jaume (p. 258),
 Toni Tort (p. 259)

Acknowledgement:
 Filipe Nunes for the coordination & layout

RCR Arquitectes Geography of Dreams
──RCRアーキテクツ　夢のジオグラフィー

2019年1月23日　初版第1刷発行

著者：RCRアーキテクツ
発行者：加藤 徹
発行所：TOTO出版（TOTO株式会社）
〒107-0062 東京都港区南青山1-24-3 TOTO乃木坂ビル2F
[営業] TEL: 03-3402-7138　FAX: 03-3402-7187
[編集] TEL: 03-3497-1010
URL: https://jp.toto.com/publishing

ブック・デザイン：spread（坂本知子、ダビッド・ロレンテ）
印刷・製本：株式会社 サンニチ印刷

落丁本・乱丁本はお取り替えいたします。
本書の全部又は一部に対するコピー・スキャン・デジタル化等の無断複製
行為は、著作権法上での例外を除き禁じます。本書を代行業者等の第三者
に依頼してスキャンやデジタル化することは、たとえ個人や家庭内での利用
であっても著作権上認められておりません。
定価はカバーに表示してあります。

© 2019 RCR Arquitectes

Printed in Japan
ISBN978-4-88706-377-8